BUSINESS ESSENTIALS B1
THE KEY SKILLS FOR ENGLISH IN THE WORKPLACE

INTRODUCTION

INTRODUCTION TO THE COURSE

WELCOME TO BUSINESS ESSENTIALS: THE ESSENTIAL LANGUAGE AND KEY PROFESSIONAL SKILLS YOU WILL NEED TO FUNCTION IN ENGLISH AT WORK.

WHAT IS IN THIS BOOK?

The book is divided into 6 modules:
- Telephone and email
- Guests and visitors
- Presenting
- Graphs and tables
- Business writing
- Job applications

Each module is divided further into 8 one-page lessons, dealing with a range of skills.

The lessons take you through a variety of business skills, and offer extensive practice opportunities. By the end of the course, you should have reached a B1 level of language proficiency.

WHAT ELSE IS THERE IN THE COURSE?

AUDIO AND VIDEO

As well as this book, there is also audio and video material accompanying the course, found on the DVD packaged with the book. The audio and video files are integrated into the course and should be accessed when you see this symbol for audio A▶3.6 or this symbol for video V▶3.

To access the video material, simply put the DVD into a DVD player or a DVD drive on your computer and choose the video clip you want to watch.

To access the audio material, put the DVD into your DVD drive on your computer, open up the DVD folder, and download the MP3 files. Or you can listen to them directly from the DVD folder.

GRAMMAR FILES

At the end of the Student's Book, you can find the Grammar Files, giving you extra grammar notes and practice of useful grammar points at B1 level.

BEC PRACTICE TEST

Also at the end of the book, there is a practice test for BEC Preliminary. Do this once you have completed Business Essentials B1, to give you some practice in the format of the BEC exam.

WHERE CAN I FIND THE ANSWER KEY?

The answer key for modules 1–6, the Grammar Files, and BEC practice test can be found at www.oup.com/elt/teacher/businessessentials.

CONTENTS

MODULE 1: TELEPHONE & EMAIL PAGE 4

- 1A Getting through on the phone
- 1B Messages and voicemails
- 1C Dealing with problems on the phone
- 1D Making arrangements on the phone
- 1E Email – first contact and requests
- 1F Email – enquiries
- 1G Email – following up
- 1H Email – levels of formality

MODULE 2: GUESTS & VISITORS PAGE 12

- 2A Introductions and greetings
- 2B Making small talk **VIDEO**
- 2C Invitations and offers
- 2D Welcoming a visitor
- 2E Understanding a welcome speech
- 2F Asking for and offering help
- 2G Telling an anecdote
- 2H Presenting yourself

MODULE 3: PRESENTING PAGE 20

- 3A A company profile **VIDEO**
- 3B Talking about your company
- 3C Company structure
- 3D Talking about your job
- 3E Talking about products
- 3F Talking about services
- 3G Talking about changes
- 3H Presenting plans **VIDEO**

MODULE 4: GRAPHS & TABLES PAGE 28

- 4A Describing graphs
- 4B Describing changes
- 4C Comparing visual information
- 4D Explaining cause and effect
- 4E Interpreting financial results
- 4F Reporting on sales figures
- 4G Describing a process
- 4H Using visuals in a presentation **VIDEO**

MODULE 5: BUSINESS WRITING PAGE 36

- 5A Introduction to emails, letters, and memos
- 5B Structuring a letter
- 5C Writing a complaint
- 5D Responding to a complaint
- 5E Placing an order
- 5F Confirming an order
- 5G Responding to an enquiry
- 5H Writing and responding to invitations

MODULE 6: JOB APPLICATIONS PAGE 44

- 6A Job ads and descriptions
- 6B Writing a CV
- 6C Writing a covering letter
- 6D Video CVs **VIDEO**
- 6E Identifying your strengths and skills
- 6F Preparing for an interview
- 6G Going to a job interview (1) **VIDEO**
- 6H Going to a job interview (2)

GRAMMAR FILES PAGE 52

BEC PRELIMINARY PRACTICE TEST PAGE 62

AUDIO AND VIDEO SCRIPTS PAGE 70

1A GETTING THROUGH ON THE PHONE

1 Discuss these questions with a partner.
1 What is difficult about using the phone in English?
2 How is it different from face-to-face communication?

2 [A▶1.1] A business journalist is writing an article about fitness centres. He wants to arrange an interview with Life Health Clubs. Listen to the phone conversation.
1 Where is the Marketing Director?
2 Why can't he speak to the Sales Director?
3 Who does he finally speak to?

3 [A▶1.1] Work with a partner and try to complete the conversation. Then listen again and check your answers.

Receptionist Life Health Clubs. How can I help?
Journalist Hi. ¹_____ George Lawrence. I'm calling from Washington. ²_____ speak to the Marketing Director, please?
Receptionist ³_____ he's in a meeting all day. Can I ⁴_____ a message, Mr Lawrence?
Journalist How about the Sales Director?
Receptionist ⁵_____ the line, please ... ⁶_____ Mr Lawrence, but his line is ⁷_____. Can I help?
Journalist Well, I'm trying to arrange a visit to your company for an article I'm writing on health clubs around the world.
Receptionist In that case I'll ⁸_____ to our Public Relations Department.

4 Put the phrases from the conversation into these categories. Add any more you can think of.

Introducing yourself

Asking to speak to someone

Apologizing

Offering to take a message

Asking the caller to wait

Saying someone is not available

Transferring someone to another person / department

5 Match phrases 1–6 with similar meanings a–f.
1 The line's busy. ____
2 Can I put you on hold? ____
3 Would you like his voicemail? ____
4 I'll put you through. ____
5 May I say who's calling? ____
6 Hold on. ____

a I'll connect you.
b One moment.
c Could I have your name?
d He's speaking to another caller.
e Would you like to wait?
f Do you want to leave a message?

6 Find five mistakes in this conversation.
A Good morning. Can I speak to Harriet Parker, please?
B Who calls, please?
A I'm Antony Phillips from the Brussels office.
B OK, I'll see if she's in ... Sorry, her line's taken. Do you want to put on hold?
A Yes, that's fine, I'll hold ...
B Hello, her line's free now. I'll connect you through.

7 Work with a partner. Role-play these two phone calls.

Student A
1 You are the caller. Call B and ask to speak to Fernando Gomez in Marketing.
2 You receive a call from B. You are the receptionist. Try to help B with his / her call. The HR Department is having an all-day departmental meeting.

Student B
1 You receive a call from A. You work in Accounts. Try to help A with his / her call.
2 You are the caller. You want to speak to the Human Resources Manager.

1B MESSAGES AND VOICEMAILS

1 Work with a partner. List some of the times and situations when you can't or don't want to answer your phone.

2 Look at the reasons why people may not be able to answer a phone call. Complete each one with one of the prepositions below.

on   at   in   off

1 They are _____ another line.
2 They are _____ holiday.
3 They are not _____ their desk.
4 They are _____ sick.
5 They are _____ a meeting.
6 They are _____ lunch.

3 **A▶1.2** Listen to four short phone conversations and answer the questions for each one.

1 Why can't the callers speak to the person they are calling?
   Call 1 _____
   Call 2 _____
   Call 3 _____
   Call 4 _____

2 What do the callers do: leave a message or say they will call back later / ask for someone to call them back?
   Call 1 _____
   Call 2 _____
   Call 3 _____
   Call 4 _____

4 **A▶1.2** Now listen again. Complete the sentences with the words used for taking and leaving messages.

1 Can I _____ a message?
2 Could you ask him to _____ me back, please?
3 Can you _____ him a message for me, then?
4 Could you _____ him I called and ask him …?
5 Shall I _____ her a message?
6 Who shall I _____ called?

5 Find six mistakes in the conversation.

Erin Could I speak to Yann, please?
Receptionist I'm afraid he's on a meeting right now. I gave him a message?
Erin This is Erin McCabe from Head Office. Can you tell to him that the meeting in Brussels has been cancelled?
Receptionist Brussels meeting cancelled …
Erin Can you ask him to call back me as soon as possible?
Receptionist No problem. Do you give me a contact number?

6 Work with a partner and follow this flow chart to role-play a phone conversation. **B** is the caller.

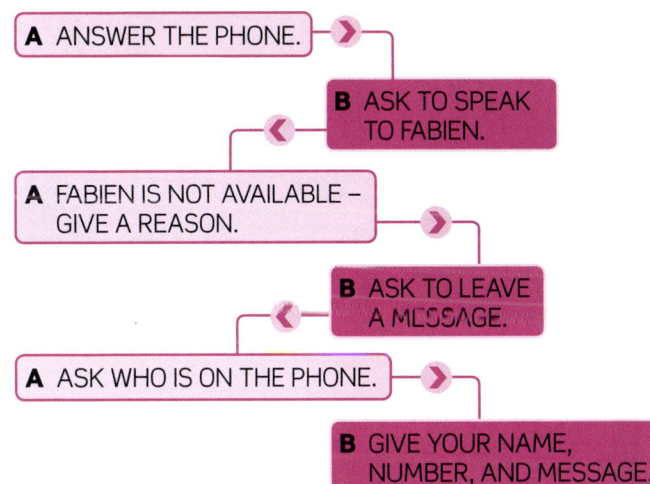

7 Put phrases a–h below into categories 1–4.

1 Leaving a contact number _____
2 Giving the time of your call _____
3 Identifying yourself _____
4 Giving a reason for the call _____

a Hi / Hello, this is …   e It's 6.30 p.m.
b Call me back on …   f You can reach me on …
c This is a message for …   g I'm calling at …
d I was just wondering if …   h I was just calling about / to …

8 **A▶1.3** In what order would you do 1–4 in **7**? Listen to a message and compare it with your answer.

9 Think of a reason for calling a colleague and note down the main points of the call you will make. Now work in groups of four – A, B, C, and D.

1 Students A and B work together, and Students C and D work together. Role-play your phone calls, asking to speak to someone, then leaving a message. Make sure you note down the message your partner leaves.

2 Now Students A and C, and Students B and D work together, and pass on the messages that you noted down.

1 TELEPHONE & EMAIL

1C DEALING WITH PROBLEMS ON THE PHONE

1 What sort of problems does this person have on the phone?

I'm sorry, can you speak more slowly, please?
Can you repeat your name, please?
I'm afraid Olympia Patel doesn't work here.
I'm afraid I can't hear you at all.
Mr Cybulska? Are you there? Mr Cybulska?

2 [A▶1.4] Listen to Kiko take a difficult call. What problems does she have? Does she deal with the problems well?

3 Complete the sentences with words for dealing with problems on the phone.
 1 I'm sorry, who's _____? Can you repeat _____, please?
 2 I'm _____, I still didn't _____ your name. Could you _____ it again, please?
 3 _____ me a _____. I've got another _____.
 4 Sorry _____ that. What can I _____ for you?
 5 I'm _____ I can't hear you.
 6 I think we got _____.
 7 Thanks. I'll _____ you straight _____.

4 Look at the phone conversations. Correct the receptionist's rude responses.
 1 **Caller** I'd like to speak to Matti, please.
   Receptionist There's no Matti here.
 2 **Caller** Ich möchte bitte mit Claudia sprechen.
   Receptionist What?
 3 **Caller** Oh hello. It's Mehmet here.
   Receptionist Who?
 4 **Caller** It's about the project.
   Receptionist Wait. I have to answer the other phone.
 5 **Caller** Hello, it's Mehmet again. We were speaking a minute ago.
   Receptionist What happened to you?
 6 **Caller** I wanted to talk to Stuart about the JW111.
   Receptionist I don't know what you're saying.

5 [A▶1.5] Now listen and check your answers.

6 Work with a partner.
Student A:
You want to make three phone calls to:
• Susan Daniels, an important client
• Henrik Andersson, a colleague in Sweden
• the Accounts Department of your stationery supplier.

Student B:
You want to make three phone calls to:
• a potential new customer
• your boss who is at another branch today
• the Human Resources Manager in your company.

Take turns making the phone calls to each other. If possible, use your actual mobile phones and call each other from different rooms.

If you are making the call, try to reach the person you want or to leave a message. If you are receiving the call, roll a dice to select one of these problems:

1 The caller says something you cannot understand.
2 It is a wrong number.
3 You do not recognize the caller.
4 You are cut off.
5 Your phone rings with another call.
6 You connect the caller to someone else in your office.

1D MAKING ARRANGEMENTS ON THE PHONE

1 Work with a partner. Look at the phrases from a phone call below. Is the conversation formal or informal?
   1 I'd like to meet you.
   2 When are you available?
   3 Does ... suit you?
   4 I'm afraid I'm not available on Tuesday.
   5 Shall we say ...?
   6 That suits me.

2 **A ▶ 1.6** Listen to Fenola Young using the language from **1** to talk to a supplier on the phone. Why and when are they meeting?

3 **A ▶ 1.7** Listen to Fenola now using more informal language to talk to a colleague, Sven. Why and when are they meeting?

4 **A ▶ 1.7** Listen again and write down the equivalent informal phrases to the formal ones from **1**.
   1 _____ for lunch next week?
   2 When _____ ?
   3 _____ Tuesday OK _____ ?
   4 Sorry, I can't _____ on Tuesday.
   5 _____ Thursday at 12.30 instead?
   6 _____ good.

5 Work with a partner and role-play the following phone calls.
   1 A supplier calling a new customer to arrange a presentation.
   2 A colleague calling another colleague to arrange a tennis match.

6 **A ▶ 1.8** Listen to the end of a phone call between a customer and a sales rep and answer questions 1–3.
   1 What do they arrange? _____
   2 What is planned for the 30th? _____
   3 What is planned for the 1st? _____

7 **A ▶ 1.8** Listen again and complete these sentences.
   1 Can we _____ a meeting then?
   2 _____ about Tuesday the 31st?
   3 I _____ the Wednesday.
   4 The 1st of February? Yes, that _____ me.

8 Work with a partner. Take turns to answer the phone and make arrangements for the situations below. Use this flow chart and your own diaries if you have them.

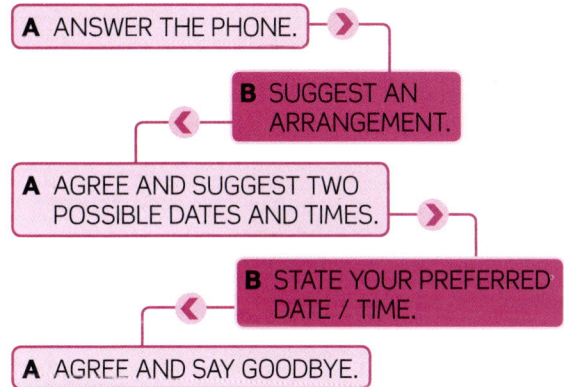

   - meeting to plan a new website
   - visiting your new company headquarters
   - celebrating your birthday
   - an anniversary dinner
   - playing golf or tennis

9 **A ▶ 1.9** Sergio calls Elena again. Listen and answer questions 1–4.
   1 What is the main reason for his call?
   2 What else do they talk about?
   3 What can't Sergio make?
   4 What do Sergio and Elena move back?

10 Read this sentence and then change the diary page below.
   'Fabio can't make the 27th, so we'll bring the meeting forward a day and move the tour back a day.'

26	27	28
	Meeting at 9.30a.m	
	Tour at 3p.m.	

11 Repeat your calls from exercise **8**, but this time you can't make the appointments. Change the arrangements to a new time. Use your own diaries if you have them.

1 TELEPHONE & EMAIL

1E EMAIL – FIRST CONTACT AND REQUESTS

1 Discuss these questions with a partner.
1. How often do you send and receive emails?
2. When do you choose to use email rather than SMS or letters?

2 Read the email and answer the questions.
1. Who is Angela?
2. Does she know Sabina Zawadzki?
3. What does Angela want?

Dear Ms Zawadzki **a**

My name is Angela Lopez, and I am a Spanish student at Western Business College. I was given your name by my tutor, Donald Kelly. **b**

I am planning a career in publishing, and I am keen to learn more about the business. I am writing to ask if there are any opportunities for work experience in your company. **c**

Thank you for your attention. I hope to hear from you soon. **d**

Regards **e**

Angela Lopez **f**

---

3 Label the parts of the email.
1. closing sentence _____
2. closing salutation _____
3. sender's name _____
4. opening salutation _____
5. reason for writing _____
6. introduction _____

4 Put these parts of an email in the correct order.

Would you like to meet for a coffee to discuss any help you might need while I am here? _____

Dear James _____

I look forward to hearing from you. _____

I have just started a work placement here and thought I would introduce myself. _____

Andrea Haussmann _____

Please let me know when you are free. _____

Best wishes _____

5 Work with a partner. Read these emails and answer the questions.
1. What is the purpose of each email?
2. Do they include all the elements in **3**? Should they?
3. How do they differ in tone?

Dear Sir or Madam

I am writing to enquire about your trainee programme. I understand you offer traineeships to business studies graduates.

I would be grateful if you could send me details of this programme.

I look forward to hearing from you.

Yours

Alex Prower

Steve

I was just wondering if you could send me the account details of JP Partnerships. I need to check an order from last year.

Thanks

Sandra

Hi Peter

I am working on a pitch for a new client and was hoping you might be able to help me. I'd be interested in seeing any examples of successful pitches you have done. Please could you send me some from the last two years?

Thanks in advance

Philip

---

6 Look back through all the emails on this page and underline any useful expressions in them. Then put the expressions into these categories.

Opening salutations
Reason for writing
Making a request
Closing sentence
Closing salutation

7 Using some of the phrases in **6**, write an email to a company asking for information on their products.

1F EMAIL - ENQUIRIES

1 Work in groups. Make a list of all the reasons why a business makes enquiries of a supplier, e.g. to ask for a brochure, to check an order.

2 Read and complete the email with these words.

| Could | recently | also | planning |
| future | know | stand | including |

> Dear Sir or Madam
>
> We saw your ¹_____ at the Montreal trade fair, and we would like to ²_____ more about your CCTV products.
>
> GFC Designs is a graphic design agency, specializing in design solutions for businesses. We have ³_____ moved to new business premises, and we are ⁴_____ to replace our security cameras in the near ⁵_____.
>
> ⁶_____ you please send us your latest catalogue, ⁷_____ a full price list? We would ⁸_____ like to know if you install and maintain your security systems.
>
> We look forward to hearing from you soon.
>
> Yours faithfully
>
> Claude Danvers

3 When you write an email, you should organize your ideas clearly. Number these items in the order you find them in 2.

a Request to reply _____
b Your enquiry _____
c Polite ending _____
d Description of your company _____
e How you know about the supplier _____

4 Work with a partner and discuss how you would reply to the email in 2. What would you include in the email?

5 Read this reply and compare it to your ideas in 4. Then answer these questions.

1 What does Ingrid send with the email?
2 What information does Ingrid ask for and why?

> Dear Mr Danvers
>
> Thank you for your enquiry. Please find attached our full, up-to-date price list. You can see our catalogue on our website by clicking on this link.
>
> I have also attached an order form, should you wish to place an order with us.
>
> I would be grateful if you could let me know where you are based, so that I can also send you details of our delivery options.
>
> If you have any further questions, please do not hesitate to ask.
>
> Yours sincerely
>
> Ingrid Mühle

6 Complete the response with appropriate words.

> Dear Ms Mühle
>
> Many thanks for getting back to me so quickly, and for supplying the ¹_____ and the ²_____.
>
> In answer to your question, my company is based in ³_____.
>
> Attached is the completed ⁴_____. I hope I have filled it in correctly.
>
> I look forward to ⁵_____ the goods.
>
> Best wishes
>
> Claude

7 Find phrases in the emails in 5 and 6 that come under these categories.

• Acknowledging someone's email
  _____

• Including separate files in the email
  _____

• Polite ending
  _____

8 Work with a partner. Each person writes an email requesting something from another company. Use some of the phrases in 7.

Then swap your emails and write a reply to your partner. Continue doing this until you feel the email exchange is at a natural end.

1 TELEPHONE & EMAIL

9

1G EMAIL – FOLLOWING UP

1 Look at these notes from a meeting and answer the questions.

1 What are the notes about?
2 What points need no further action?
3 What still needs to be done for the other points?
4 Which of the points will Elaine be taking on herself?

> **Conference planning meeting 20/03**
> **Update from Elaine:**
> 1 **Venue:** booked – Sheldon conference centre.
> 2 **Accommodation for delegates:** Still trying to negotiate deals with local hotels.
> 3 **Speakers:** All but two have confirmed. Need to chase up these two.
> 4 **Catering:** Have received quotes from three suppliers. **Action point:** circulate quotes to team.
> 5 **Sponsorship:** no action yet taken, volunteer needed to take this on.
> 6 **Publicity:** Freelancer to create flyers. Need to check availability.

2 Read these email extracts from Elaine. Which points from the meeting do they address?

1

> Dear Mr Carson
> Further to our conversation last week, I wonder if I could press you on a decision as to whether you will speak at our conference in June.

2

> Dear all
> Following on from our meeting yesterday, here are the three quotes I talked about. Please take a look and let me know what you think. Please note that I am still expecting two more quotes as well.

3

> Hi Tania
> As you know, in the conference planning meeting yesterday it was agreed that I would need to get some help with one of the tasks. I was told you had a bit of spare time at the moment. Is that the case?
> I'm copying in Amanda so she is aware I'm asking you for your time.

3 All of the emails above are following up on a previous discussion or meeting. Find phrases in the emails that mean the following:

1 As we discussed in …
_____
_____
_____

2 This is extra / new information:
_____

3 I'm letting [someone else] read this email …
_____

4 We decided that …
_____

4 [A ▶ 1.10] Elaine has found a freelancer to make the flyers for the conference. Listen to a phone conversation they have and answer the questions.

1 When does Harriet have to finish the flyer?
2 What is Elaine going to do next?
3 What do they agree on at the end of the conversation?

5 Write two follow-up emails from Elaine.

1 Write to the Sheldon Hotel to confirm the conference booking.
2 Write to Harriet, the flyer designer, confirming her job and attaching the job details. You also want your boss, Fiona Porter, to know about this.

6 When you have written your two emails, compare them with a partner's. Did you both include the same things in your emails? Do you have any advice on how to improve them?

1H EMAIL – LEVELS OF FORMALITY

1 Look at the pieces of advice about writing emails. Which ones do you agree with? Discuss your answers with a partner.

Emails follow most of the rules of business letter writing.

Always use an appropriate ending.

Always use an appropriate greeting at the start.

Use complete words – don't use contractions or abbreviations.

Use complete sentences.

2 Decide which of the following are formal [F], informal [I] or can be found in both situations [B].

Yours faithfully _____
Dear Mr Dunne _____
Best wishes _____
Yours sincerely _____
All the best _____
Thank you for your enquiry. _____
Please contact us if you have any further enquiries. _____
How are you? _____
Take care. _____
We look forward to hearing from you. _____
It's me again! _____
Dear Sir or Madam _____
Looking forward to the meeting. _____
Hi Sam _____
See you soon! _____
Regards _____

3 Read these emails and answer the questions.
1 In email a, what does Bruno ask Colette to do?
2 In email b, what information does Colette add?
3 In email c, what information does the hotel request?
4 In email d, what does Colette offer to do?
5 Which emails are more informal and why?
6 What do the abbreviations btw, FYI, and asap mean?

a

Colette

Thanks for booking the meeting with the Du Pont clients. Could you book me a room at the Park Inn Hotel, Geneva for the three nights? The usual – non-smoking, quiet double room!

Thanks

Bruno

btw: Do you know if Claire is going too?

b

Dear Sir or Madam

I am writing to enquire if you have a double room, single occupancy, available for three nights, 27th, 28th and 29th March, for Mr Bruno Levy. He requires a non-smoking, quiet room.

I look forward to hearing from you.

Yours faithfully

Colette Montand
Personal Assistant

c

Dear Colette Montand

We have a double room for the nights you require. It is a quiet room at the back of the hotel and is on a non-smoking corridor. The price is 300 Swiss francs per night, including breakfast.

The hotel has security-controlled parking for an extra 25 Swiss francs per day.

We will hold the booking for 48 hours but we require your credit card number to confirm it.

Please could you also inform us if Mr Levy requires parking.

Yours sincerely

Carlo Graf

d

Bruno

FYI – I've booked the hotel.

Do you want me to book you a parking space at the hotel too? I need to get back to them asap on this.

Colette

4 You are Colette. Write the following emails.
1 Write to the hotel: confirm the booking and give credit card details (VISA 6783 2612 4382 9032, expiry date: 06/15). Bruno doesn't need a parking space.
2 Write to Bruno asking him when he wants to travel to Geneva.
3 Write to the hotel: book another room for Sophie Meyer.
4 Write to Bruno asking him if you should book a train ticket for Sophie.

2A INTRODUCTIONS AND GREETINGS

1 Work with a partner and discuss these questions.
   1 How many different ways of greeting people are there in your country? What do people do in other countries?
   2 What do you find easy or difficult about introducing yourself to other people in English?

2 **A▶2.1** Gianluca Donatelli is at a conference. Listen to him introducing himself to Jana Frkova. Make notes about:
   1 Jana's nationality
   2 her job
   3 why she's at the conference.

3 **A▶2.1** Complete what Gianluca says. Then listen and check your answers.
   1 Excuse me. _____ this seat free?
   2 Thanks very much. Can I _____ myself? I'm Gianluca Donatelli.
   3 Nice to meet you _____, Jana. Where are you _____?
   4 And _____ do you work for?
   5 Oh really? And what do you _____?
   6 So _____ are you at this conference?
   7 That's interesting. A friend of mine works for an Italian service provider. Can I introduce _____ to _____?
   8 Roberto. Can you come here for a minute? This is … Sorry, what's your name _____?
   9 Roberto. _____ is Jana. She's writing an article on Internet service providers.

4 **A▶2.2** Listen to two extracts from a different version of the conversation.
   1 What do we learn about Gianluca this time?
   2 Underline the stressed words in Jana's questions.
      a What about you? What do you do?
      b What about you? What are you here for?

5 Rachel Steadman meets Gideon Lack at an international car show. Complete the conversation below with sentences a–i.
   a Nice to meet you too,
   b Can I introduce you to her?
   c And what do you do?
   d what's your name again?
   e What about you?
   f This is Rachel.
   g Can I introduce myself?
   h Nice to meet you.
   i What does the company do?

Rachel Excuse me. Can I sit here?
Gideon Yes, of course.
Rachel Thanks very much. ¹_____ I'm Rachel Steadman.
Gideon ²_____ I'm Gideon Lack.
Rachel ³_____ Gideon. Where are you from?
Gideon I'm from Switzerland originally. But I live in Germany now. ⁴_____ Where are you based?
Rachel In Toronto.
Gideon And who do you work for?
Rachel Bos. Perhaps you don't know it.
Gideon No, I don't. ⁵_____
Rachel It's an advertising agency. I'm here with Honda. It's one of our clients. ⁶_____
Gideon I'm a teacher of Greek literature.
Rachel Oh really? What brings you to this car show?
Gideon I'm here with my wife. She works for BMW. Ah, there she is now. ⁷_____
Rachel Yes, of course. That would be nice.
Gideon Sorry, ⁸_____
Rachel Rachel. Rachel Steadman.
Gideon Ursula. ⁹_____ She works for an advertising agency in Canada.

6 Work with a partner. Imagine you are at a social event at a conference. Complete details about yourself on this role card.

> Name: _____
> Job: _____
> Company: _____
> Reason for being here: _____

Introduce yourself to your partner using the phrases you have just learned. Then introduce your partner to someone else in the group.

2B MAKING SMALL TALK

1 Work with a partner. Look at the topics below. Which ones is it normal to talk about in your country when you meet someone from abroad for the first time?

work   the journey   money   the visitor's country
family   politics   interests   holidays

2 **A▶2.3** Listen to Dan Ford meeting Jozef Dropinski at the airport. Which topics from 1 do they talk about?

3 **A▶2.3** Complete the questions from the conversation in 2 with *do*, *did*, or *are*. Then listen and check your answers.
1 _____ you have a good flight?
2 _____ you often travel abroad on business?
3 _____ you see the Alhambra?
4 What _____ you think of it?
5 _____ you interested in architecture?
6 When _____ you usually take your holiday?

4 Complete the table with the questions in 3.

Asking about a journey	Asking about experiences
How was your journey?	Is this your first time in Tokyo?
Was the flight delayed?	Have you been here before?
_____	_____

Asking about habits	Asking about opinions / interests
Do you ever go skiing?	What kind of music do you like?
_____	_____
_____	_____

5 Work with a partner. Using some of the phrases in the table in 4, make three questions to ask your partner. Then take turns asking and answering them.

6 **V▶1** In this video, Maria has just started a new job. Watch the video and answer the questions.
1 What is Maria waiting for?
2 What do Maria and Monica talk about?
3 What are their jobs?
4 What do they have in common?

7 **V▶1** Maria and Monica keep their conversation going by asking each other questions and showing interest. Watch again and make a note of the questions they ask.

Maria	
Monica	

8 Think of three more questions you could ask a new colleague to find out more about them or the company. Work with a partner and have a short conversation. Start off by using your questions, then keep the conversation going with some follow-up questions. Use the flow chart below to help you if necessary.

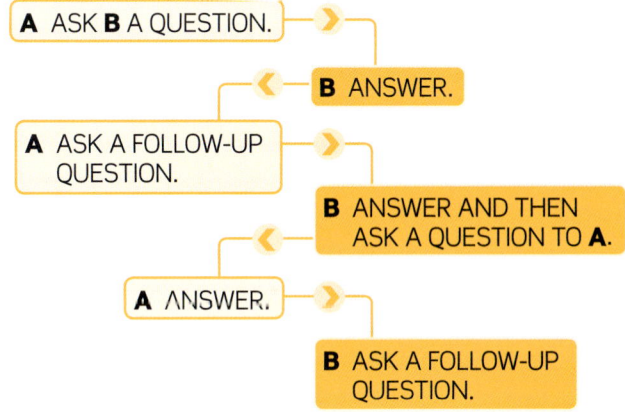

9 When you have finished your conversation, tell the rest of the class what you found out about your partner.

2 GUESTS & VISITORS

2C INVITATIONS AND OFFERS

1 ▶2.4 Listen to four conversations and match each one with a place a–d.
a Outside a hotel ___
b In a manager's office ___
c In a company reception ___
d By a hot drinks machine ___

2 ▶2.4 Complete invitations and offers 1–4 and responses a–d from the conversations. Then match each invitation or offer to a response. Listen again and check your answers.

1 _____ join us?
2 _____ get you a glass of water?
3 _____ a coffee?
4 _____ book a ticket for you?

a Yes, please. That's very _____ of you.
b No, thanks. I'd _____ have tea.
c Yes, please. That would be _____.
d Thanks for the _____, but …

3 Put the phrases in **2** into these categories.

Inviting	
Offering	
Accepting	
Declining	

4 Are these ways of offering something formal, informal, or neutral?
1 Would you like a drink?
2 Do you want a drink?
3 Do you fancy a drink?
4 Can I get you a drink?

5 ▶2.5 Complete these responses to the offers in **4** with words from the list. Then listen to six conversations and check your answers.

would   sounds   fine   time   love   please

1 No thanks, I'm _____.
2 I'd _____ one.
3 Yes, _____.
4 A drink _____ good.
5 That _____ be great, thanks.
6 I'm afraid I don't have _____.

6 Work with a partner. Look at these situations and take turns to make and respond to invitations and offers, using the phrases above.
1 Your visitor is looking tired.
2 Your visitor doesn't have enough copies of a document she needs for her talk.
3 It's the opening night of *Madame Butterfly*. Your visitor loves opera.
4 The meeting is over and your visitor's hotel is on the other side of town.
5 It's lunchtime and your visitor hasn't eaten since breakfast at 8.00.
6 Your visitor wants to set up a PowerPoint presentation, but they need help.

7 Work with a partner and role-play the situations below.

Student A

Role-play 1: Student B is a potential client who has spent the day visiting your company. Your colleagues have booked a table at a restaurant for dinner. Invite him / her and say when and where the table is booked. Offer to pick him / her up from the hotel.

Role-play 2: You are a colleague of Student B's in a different branch. You are spending the day in meetings at Student B's branch. You have a very busy day, but are free in the evening.

Student B

Role-play 1: You are a potential client of Student A's. You have spent the day at his / her company.

Role-play 2: Student A is a colleague at a different branch and is spending the day in meetings at your branch. You see Student A in the morning. Invite him / her to lunch. Offer to help with any work Student A has to do. Try to find a time when you can meet for a meal or a drink.

2D WELCOMING A VISITOR

1 When someone comes to visit your place of work, what do you show them? Are there any areas which are 'off-limits' (private or secret)?

2 ▶ 2.6 Jacinta Ross works for JJP Electronics. She meets Marvin Bernstein at reception. He is visiting the company for the day. Listen to their conversation and complete the agenda for Marvin's visit.

Agenda for Marvin Bernstein's visit to JJP Electronics
Monday, 2 October

Morning:

Lunchtime:

Afternoon:

3 ▶ 2.6 Listen again and complete these phrases that Jacinta uses.

1 _____ our new facility.
2 It's nice to _____ in person.
3 So, how was _____?
4 And did you have _____ finding us?
5 Here, _____ your coat.
6 Can I _____ a coffee?
7 OK. Come this way and I'll _____ today's programme.
8 So, first of all, I _____ join a tour of the facility this morning.
9 Then, _____ at lunchtime.
10 He's introducing the tour this morning, but _____ to meet up with him over lunch.
11 You'll need this ID card to get around the site. _____ you keep it on you at all times.
12 Yes, _____ that. I'll clear it with Facilities.

4 Work with a partner. Match these responses to phrases 1–8 in 3.

a Likewise. ____
b Thank you. ____
c OK. ____
d That sounds interesting. ____
e Yes, please. Black, no sugar. ____
f I'll hang on to it, thanks. ____
g Not really, it was easy. ____
h It was fine, thanks. ____

5 Work with a partner. Have a conversation with a visitor to your place of work using this flow chart. Student A is the visitor and Student B is the host. When you have finished, change roles.

A INTRODUCE YOURSELF TO B.
B IDENTIFY YOURSELF AND WELCOME A.
A RESPOND.
B ASK ABOUT A'S JOURNEY.
A RESPOND.
B OFFER TEA, COFFEE, ETC.
A RESPOND.
B TALK ABOUT SCHEDULE.
A RESPOND AND ASK TO MEET ANOTHER COLLEAGUE.
B RESPOND.

6 Work with a partner. Imagine you are welcoming a new person to the class today.

Have a short conversation about their journey to the classroom and go through the schedule for the lesson.

2 GUESTS & VISITORS

2E UNDERSTANDING A WELCOME SPEECH

1 Work with a partner and discuss the following questions.
  1 Have you ever made a welcome speech at a conference or a party? If so, were you happy with it?
  2 Have you been to a conference or a party where you heard a welcome speech? Was it good? Why? / Why not?

2 Read this welcome speech. What is the reason for the event?

> 1 Ladies and gentlemen, welcome to the official opening of our new headquarters. It's lovely to see so many of our colleagues from around the world here tonight.
>
> 2 As you know, our company started twelve years ago in a small rented office in Berlin. Since then, we have opened offices around the world and now employ over 500 people. The opening of this office is the next step in our expansion.
>
> 3 Before we begin the celebrations, I'd like to thank the organizers of this event, Janet Merrion and Howard Duncan, for doing such an excellent job. I'm sure you'll all agree that the dinner menu looks delicious and the entertainment programme is fantastic.
>
> 4 We're also honoured to have leading sports personality Friedrich Neff from the Hertha Berlin football team with us this evening.
>
> 5 While you're here, please feel free to look around the building and if you have any questions, please speak to any member of staff. Now, before I hand you over to Friedrich Neff to cut the ribbon and open the champagne, I'd like to thank you all once again for being here and I hope you enjoy the evening.

3 Work with a partner. Look at the welcome speech again and match sections 1–5 to functions a–e.
  a Talk about the reason for the event: ___
  b Thank people who have helped to organize the event: ___
  c Wish everyone a good day / good evening: ___
  d Give a special welcome to important guests: ___
  e Greet everyone: ___

4 Match 1–6 to a–f to make complete sentences.
  1 It's lovely … ___
  2 We're honoured … ___
  3 I'm sure you'll all agree that … ___
  4 I'd like to thank my wonderful PA, Janice Holder, … ___
  5 Before I hand you over to Sir David, … ___
  6 I hope … ___

  a the event programme looks fantastic.
  b you enjoy the party.
  c for organizing the fantastic buffet.
  d to see so many of you here tonight.
  e I'd like to thank you all once again for coming.
  f to have Sir David Morrow with us this evening.

5 [A ▶ 2.7] Listen to a different welcome speech and answer the questions.
  1 Who is Dilip Patel?
  2 How is the day organized?
  3 What piece of advice does Dilip give the visitors?

6 Which elements from **3** are included in this speech? What other elements are in this speech?

7 [A ▶ 2.7] Listen again and find formal equivalents to these phrases.
  1 Welcome to …
  2 You'll get a chance to …
  3 Remember …
  4 Make sure you …

8 Work in groups of two or three. Write a welcome speech for an event of your own choice.

9 Take turns to give your welcome speech to the class. As you listen to the other welcome speeches, make a note of what the event is for and any special instructions the speakers give. Check whether everyone used all the functions in **3**.

2F ASKING FOR AND OFFERING HELP

1 Imagine you have just started a new job. What things might you need help with at first? Make a list with a partner.

2 Read these emails from a new member of staff, asking for help. Underline the phrases she uses to introduce the request for help. Which phrases are formal and which are informal?

> Hi Patrick
>
> Thanks for your help this morning with setting up my desk. However, my phone still isn't working. Can you spare a moment to come and see if you can fix it?
>
> Thanks
>
> Carla

> Dear Ms Foster
>
> I wonder if you could help me with something. I have just started today and I need to access the customer database. Could I ask you to help me with the initial set-up at some point this week?
>
> Many thanks
>
> Carla Dubrowka

> Hello Frieda
>
> I'm your new colleague in the department. I hope we can meet soon for a coffee. In the meantime, can I ask a favour? I could do with some help with order processing. Is there a handbook for this, or could you show me how to do it?
>
> Thanks in advance
>
> Carla

3 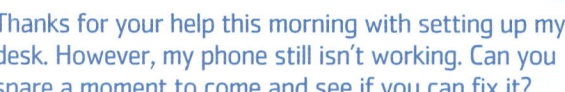 Fran and John work for a travel guide publisher. They have a stand at a trade fair in London. Read the sentences below, and then listen to four short conversations. Correct the information in the sentences. One of the sentences is already correct.

1 Fran cannot find the books on Australia.
2 Fran thinks there is space in the car for everything.
3 Fran has made a mistake with her T-shirt.
4 Fran does not want to go to the pub.

4 Put the words from the conversations in the correct order. Then listen again and check your answers.

1 want / help / you / do / some?
2 them / just / I'll / get.
3 help / me / let.
4 me / to / it / leave.
5 OK / doing / you / are?
6 want / hand / you / do / a?
7 can / how / help / I?
8 get / for / one / shall / you / I?

5 Put the sentences above into the correct category.

A Asking if someone needs help: ____, ____, ____
B Offering to do something: ____, ____, ____
C Stating you want to help: ____, ____

6 The table below shows a list of possible responses to asking for or offering help. Label the phrases A (response to someone asking for help) or O (response to an offer of help).

Positive responses	Negative responses
Yes please, that would be good.	I'm afraid I'm a bit busy.
Yes, no problem.	No I'm fine, thanks.
Yes, thanks.	I'll be OK, thanks.
That's kind of you, thanks.	I can't really help with that. Sorry.
Yes, of course.	I can manage.
Yes, what can I do?	Sorry, I don't know the answer to that.

7 Look back at the list you made in 1. Role-play some of the situations with a partner. Use the expressions for offering and asking for help on this page.

2G TELLING AN ANECDOTE

1 Do you prefer to tell an interesting story or listen to one? Why?

2 Look at these pictures. In which situations might you want to be able to tell a story or describe an event? Explain your choices.

3 **A▶2.9** Mark, Gina, and Simon are talking during a coffee break at their office in New York. Simon has just started telling them a story about a time that he was travelling. Listen and answer the questions.

1 Why was Simon in London?
2 What was the problem at Heathrow Airport?
3 What did the airline staff ask the passengers?
4 What did Simon say?

4 **A▶2.10** What do you think happened to Simon after this? Discuss your ideas in small groups. Then listen to the next part of his story and check if you were right.

5 **A▶2.9** Listen again to the earlier part of the conversation. Correct the sentences with the right verb forms for telling a story.

1 I was in London a few years ago on a business trip, and I flew back home ...
2 I could see these two ground staff ... they came down the line.
3 Well, I can see that there were families on vacation ...
4 ... and they probably have had a tighter schedule than me.
5 And I went home, so a day earlier, a day later, what the heck.
6 No, I was saying: 'It would be very inconvenient for me ...'

6 Read this extract from a presentation given by a visitor to another company. Complete it with the correct form of the verb.

> Several years ago, I ¹_____ (visit) your company for the first time. At the time I ²_____ (work) in France, so I ³_____ (come) by train. As you know, back then, you ⁴_____ (build) this magnificent building that we are in today, and I ⁵_____ (can) see the building work as the train ran alongside this site. It's really wonderful to see it finally ...

7 Work with a partner. Think of your journey into work or school this morning. Tell your partner about it using the correct forms of the past tense.

8 **A▶2.10** Simon uses some phrases to help keep his audience's attention. Put the words in the right order. Then listen again to the final part of the conversation and check your answers.

1 guess / and / what
_____

2 so / told / them / I
_____

3 finished / not / on / I'm / yet / hang
_____

4 do / think / what / you?
_____

9 Work in small groups. Spend a few minutes thinking about a time you were travelling when something interesting happened. Make notes about these points:

- Where were you travelling to / from?
- Why were you travelling?
- What was the interesting incident?
- How did you feel?
- Who did you talk to?
- How was it resolved?
- How did you feel afterwards?

10 Take turns to tell your anecdote to your group. Try to keep your audience's attention by using some of the phrases in **8**.

2H PRESENTING YOURSELF

1 ▶2.11 Listen to two people, Thorsten Richter and Amy Chang, giving a presentation about themselves at the beginning of their talk at a company conference. Who gives the most information about themselves?

2 ▶2.11 Listen again. Which speaker says the following?
1 Last year I was promoted to this position.
2 I studied economics and business.
3 Recently I have worked on several successful cases.
4 In my previous role I ran the Creative Department in Bonn.
5 Up to now I've managed to find solutions for all the companies I have worked with.
6 Over the last year I've met with all the country managers.
7 In my current role as consultant to your company, I'm looking to improve your sales figures.
8 At the moment we're working together with a consultant.
9 Over the next year I'll spend two weeks in each department.
10 In the future we may have to target a different market.

3 Complete the table with the time phrases in 2.

Talking about the past
Last year
Talking about recent experiences
Talking about the present
Talking about the future

4 Read this presentation by a guest trainer at a company. Complete it with phrases from the list.

at the moment   In the future   In my previous role
Last year   Up to now   Over the next week

> Right then, before I start, I'll tell you a bit about myself and my organization. My name's Amjad Kazalbash and I run the Star School of Management. ¹_____ I was a manager in a successful electronics company. Later I decided to open a school to train future managers.
> ²_____ my colleagues and I have given courses in nearly a hundred different companies, and all of our clients have gone away satisfied.
> ³_____ I took on five new trainers which means there are twenty highly-qualified professionals working at my school ⁴_____.
> ⁵_____ we hope to develop even more training courses. But, for now, I hope you'll find the sessions useful.
> ⁶_____ I will be supervising the course and answering any questions you may have about the material. So now, let me introduce you to your trainer ...

5 Work with a partner. Arjan Holtmann, a management consultant, is going to give a talk at your company. You have been asked to introduce him to the group. Prepare a short presentation about him using this information.

Arjan Holtmann
Management Consultant

Professional background
Managing Director, Karpinsky Ltd, 1999–2012
Recent experience
Advising small companies on how to expand
Present role
Head of AH Consulting
Plans for the future
To expand AH Consulting into other markets – Belgium, Germany, Austria.

6 Practise giving your introduction about Arjan using phrases from 3 and 4.

7 Now prepare and give a presentation about yourself to the class. Include:
- your education
- your work experience
- your recent experiences
- your present situation

2 GUESTS & VISITORS

3A A COMPANY PROFILE

PRESENTING 3

1 Work with a partner. Make a list of all the things you would expect to find out about a company if you were reading or listening to a company profile.

2 Are you able to give correct information on the items in your list about your school or company?

3 [V▶2] Watch the interview with a company director. Number the topics in the order he talks about them (1–6).
   a Glasbau Hahn's competitors _____
   b The history of the company _____
   c Glasbau Hahn's products _____
   d Where Glasbau Hahn is based _____
   e Key markets _____
   f Company employees _____

4 Are there any areas from your list in **1** that Till doesn't mention?

5 [V▶2] Make more detailed notes about each of the areas in **3**. Then compare them with a partner. Watch the video again and check your notes.

6 Write down what these numbers refer to in the video. Read the transcript on page 73 to check your answers.
   a 1836 _____
   b 3 _____
   c 6 _____
   d 120 _____
   e 15 _____
   f 1970 _____

7 Read this company profile. Are these sentences true (T) or false (F)?
   1 The company has always been in the food business. _____
   2 It has a limited range of products. _____
   3 It tries to get products from all over the world. _____
   4 All of its business is in Europe. _____
   5 It has been sold several times since it began. _____

> J. Canning Ltd is a family company. It was founded in 1894 by Joseph Canning, who began by selling bread and baked goods from a street stall.
>
> It now sells a huge range of food goods to restaurants, shops, and hotels. Its unique selling proposition is that it sources food locally and, therefore, has a lower impact on the environment than its competitors.
>
> It employs over 2,500 people and has 3 offices in the UK, including its head office in Birmingham.
>
> 85% of its business is in the UK, while 15% is in northern European markets, such as Denmark and the Netherlands.
>
> The company has expanded since it started, but it is still run by the Canning family – Joseph's great-grandson, Patrick, is the current CEO.

8 Find words in the text in **7** to match these definitions.
   1 country or countries where products are sold _____
   2 something that makes it different _____
   3 started _____
   4 finds _____
   5 effect _____
   6 got bigger _____
   7 managed _____
   8 head of a company _____

9 Work with a partner. Think of reasons why it might be useful or important to know about a company before you start doing business with them. What could go wrong if you don't know anything about them?

10 Now, with the same partner, try to agree on the three most important factors when buying a product. For example: quality, cost, time taken to manufacture / import the product, company reputation. Think of your own examples too.

11 Next, compare your ideas with another pair. Discuss your answers as a group and try to agree on the three most important factors. Give reasons for your choices.

20

3B TALKING ABOUT YOUR COMPANY

1 Work with a partner. Think of a company in your region or country. How much do you know about it? Make a list of facts about the company.

2 Read these descriptions of some companies. Complete their names.
1 This company **provides** many different Internet services including news, online shopping, and email. Most of its **sales** come from advertising on its website. Its head office is in Sunnyvale, California. Y_____
2 This company **produces** tyres for cars and other vehicles. It is **based** in France, but it has more than 125,000 **employees** all over the world. It is also well known for its red and green travel guides. M_____
3 This northern European company operates in the retail market. It **specializes** in low-price products, including furniture, bathrooms, and kitchens. I_____
4 It's a **subsidiary** of the European Aeronautic Defence and Space Company (EADS). The company makes planes for the commercial aircraft market, where its main **competitor** is Boeing. A_____
5 This company makes many different electrical and electronic products, such as TVs, computers, and mobile phones. It is South Korea's largest company and exporter. S_____

3 Complete these sentences with a form of the words in bold in **2**.
1 Some companies make or _____ goods.
2 Other companies _____ or offer services.
3 If you _____ in a particular product or service, it's your main activity.
4 If you work for a company, you are an _____.
5 If your head office is in a particular city, your company is _____ there.
6 If you work in a _____, your company is part of a bigger group.
7 If you sell a lot of products, your _____ are very good.
8 If another company operates in the same market as you, it is your _____.

4 Work with a partner. Make sentences using the words in the table.

Gazprom	produces / makes ...
Pirelli	specializes in ...
AOL	operates in ...
Mitsubishi	provides / offers ...
Volkswagen	sells ...
UNICEF	's competitors are ...

5 A ▶ 3.1 An employee is talking about her company. Listen and complete the information in the table.

Name of company	Besam
Products	[1]A_____ [2]d_____ mechanisms: locks and [3]s_____ systems
Group	Assa Abloy
Nationality	[4]S_____
Number of employees	[5]_____,000
Sales	€[6]_____ billion
Number of subsidiaries	[7]_____ in 40 countries
Other information	Main [8]c_____ are the Eastern Company, Ingersoll Rand, and Master Lock

6 Work with a partner. Talk about Besam, using some or all of these phrases and the information in **5**.

It's a(n) ... company
It's a subsidiary of ...
Its head office is ...
It makes / produces ...
It provides / offers ...
It has ... employees
It operates in ...
It is based in ...
It specializes in ...
Its main competitors are ...
It has sales of ...

7 Work with a partner. Take turns describing a well-known company using the phrases in **6**. Don't tell your partner which company you are describing. Your partner must guess.

3 PRESENTING

21

3C COMPANY STRUCTURE

1 Look at this list of common company departments. Discuss with a partner what each one does. Are there any other departments you would add to the list?

Sales   Marketing   Purchasing   Finance
Research and Development   Training   IT
Production   Logistics   Quality Control
Human Resources   Customer Services
Technical Support

2 Which department usually:
1 sells the products?
2 does the advertising and communication?
3 creates new products?
4 answers technical questions from customers?
5 answers all other questions from customers?

3 Complete the sentences about other departments with words from the list.

finds   buys   checks   arranges
maintains   deals   organizes

1 The Logistics Department _____ the transport of products.
2 The Training Department _____ courses.
3 The Purchasing Department _____ from suppliers.
4 The Human Resources Department _____ new staff.
5 The IT Department _____ the computer system.
6 The Finance Department _____ with all the money.
7 The Quality Control Department _____ that the products have no defects.

4 Work with a partner. Take turns to make sentences about different people who work in a company and to guess which department they work in.

Example:
A She deals with all the money.
B She works in the Finance Department.

5 A ▶ 3.2 Three people are receiving visitors from other departments in their company. Listen to the three conversations and complete the table.

Person	Which department does he /she work in?	Which department does his / her visitor work in?
1		
2		
3		

6 A ▶ 3.2 Listen again and complete these sentences.
1 I have a meeting today with Anna Neves, who's _____ our software.
2 Our company is _____ three business units.
3 He's the person in _____ buying for the whole group.
4 I _____ a lot of training organizations.
5 I _____ the HR Director.

7 Look at this company organization chart and complete the sentences with a suitable word or words.

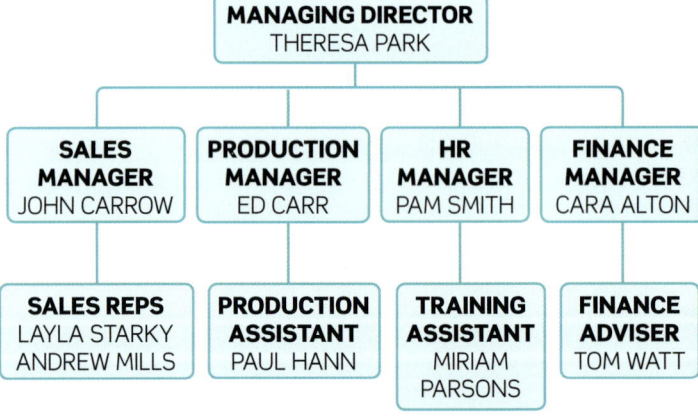

1 Ed _____ the MD.
2 Cara _____ for looking after the books.
3 Miriam _____ training courses.
4 Tom _____ the accounts.
5 Theresa _____ of the entire company.

8 Work with a partner. Add more departments and roles to the organization chart above, or create your own. Then take turns describing the roles and responsibilities of each person / department.

3D TALKING ABOUT YOUR JOB

1 What do you think these people do in their work?
   1 a retail buyer
   2 a public relations officer
   3 an occupational psychologist

2 Read the texts quickly and compare your answers to 1.

1 Sara – Retail Buyer

I work for a supermarket chain. My job **involves** buying prepared salads and vegetables from local and national *suppliers*. I also **take part in** different logistics projects. For example, at the moment we're working with an external *consultant*. He's looking at ways to get our salads and vegetables to the supermarket shelves more quickly.

2 Benjamin – Public Relations Officer

I work for the police, but I'm not a police officer. A lot of my work **consists of** answering questions from journalists when the police are in the news. I'm also **involved in** a new project to attract new people to the police force. For this, I'm working with senior police officers and with outside *employment agencies*.

3 Heidi – Occupational Psychologist

I'm self-employed. Basically, I **deal with** problems of relations between *staff*. At the moment, for example, I'm doing a study on virtual teamwork for one of my industrial *customers*. They work with many *subcontractors* all over the world, and their managers want to communicate better with their *colleagues* abroad. I work a lot with *training organizations* which provide the courses my customers need.

3 Read the texts again and answer these questions. Which person or people:
   1 work(s) on problems of communication? _____
   2 work(s) with people outside the company? _____
   3 work(s) with products? _____
   4 work(s) with companies, but not for a company? _____

4 Work with a partner. Match the words in *italics* in the texts to definitions a–h.
   a companies which sell their products to you
   b organizations which find new employees for you
   c companies which do work for you which you can't do yourself
   d people who work in the same company as you
   e organizations which offer courses to company employees
   f a person from outside a company who gives expert advice
   g companies which buy your products
   h all the people who work for a company

5 **A▶3.3** Sang Chun is talking about his job in a software company. Listen and tick (✔) the people that he works with and the jobs that he does.

People	Jobs
Customers	Answering calls
Suppliers	Visiting
Sales reps	Developing new programs
Programmers	Discussing old programs

6 **A▶3.3** Complete this description of Sang Chun's job with a form of the phrases in **bold** from the texts in 2. Listen again and check your answers.

MAIN JOB
This ¹_____ answering calls from customers who are having problems with their software. It also ²_____ working with sales reps from time to time.

OTHER TASKS
He isn't ³_____ developing new programs. But when programmers are preparing new versions of old products, he ⁴_____ in the discussions.

TYPICAL PROBLEMS
He ⁵_____ installation issues, password problems, bugs, etc.

7 Work with a partner. Tell your partner about your job. If you do not have a job, think of a job you have had or would like to have. What is similar to your partner's job and what is different?
   • Main job
   • Typical problems
   • Other tasks (projects, etc.)
   • People you work with inside and outside the company

3 PRESENTING

3E TALKING ABOUT PRODUCTS

1 What new products can you buy at the moment? Think about the following areas.
- electronic gadgets
- food and drink
- health and beauty

2 Write the names of your favourite brands for the products or services below. Then discuss the reasons you prefer them.
- shoes _____
- mobile phone _____
- coffee _____
- airline _____

3 Do you often try new products or do you usually keep to one brand?

4 Look at texts 1–4, which describe four new products. Match the texts to pictures a–d.

1 A **well-designed** piece of office furniture. Comes with **user-friendly** assembly instructions.

2 A simple and **functional** item. Frequent travellers like it as it is **compact** and can fit easily into a washbag or overnight bag.

3 Travel in style with this brand new **stylish** and **attractive**, yet **practical**, item.

4 If you haven't already made the switch, do it now, if only because it's more **economical**.

5 Match 1–8 below to definitions a–h.
1 practical   a costs less to run
2 economical   b easy to use
3 attractive   c fashionable and good to look at
4 functional   d useful
5 stylish   e small
6 user-friendly   f useful with little decoration
7 well-designed   g beautiful
8 compact   h planned and made well

6 Complete these sentences with words in **bold** from the texts in **4**.
1 Our carpooling system is much cheaper for the staff. It's more _____.
2 Our new car is much easier to park. It's very _____ for driving in the city centre.
3 The new reception area looks more modern. It's quite _____.
4 They took a long time planning the new model. It's very _____.
5 The new office furniture is exactly what we needed. It's very _____.
6 The operating system on my computer is easy to use. It's very _____.
7 Jack's new PDA fits in his pocket. It's quite _____.
8 I really like our new uniforms. They're really _____.

7 Work with a partner. Take turns to describe different products you have or use, for example, your mobile phone, car, coat, bag, or PC.

Example:
My car wasn't cheap, but it is very economical because it doesn't use much petrol.

8 Work in a small group. Imagine your company is launching a new product. Decide what the product is, then prepare a short presentation about it. Present the product to your class, using the ideas below to help you.
- product or service brand
- product or service development
- description of the product or service

3F TALKING ABOUT SERVICES

1 Work with a partner. Discuss these questions.
  1 What services do you use regularly? Make a list.
  2 What do you like about them?
  3 What makes services good or bad?

2 Read these website reviews.
  1 Which of the extracts is about a website for
   • a bank?
   • a newspaper?
   • an online travel agency?
  2 Would you be interested in these services? Why? / Why not?

a
> Instead of continuously visiting websites to see if there are new articles and updates, you can have them delivered directly to you. Its user-friendly service gives you access to all the most up-to-date and accurate news and information on the web.

b
> This service is free and gives you immediate access to your accounts when it's convenient for you. The system also protects your personal financial information and ensures that you stay secure.

c
> This system is really time-saving and efficient, because consumers can combine multiple flights, hotel bookings, car rentals, and local activities all from just one website. Users can customize their bookings to fit their needs and there are many discounts and special prices, so it's really cost-effective.

3 A ▶ 3.4 Listen to three speakers. Which website in 2 would they be interested in?

4 Underline the adjectives in the reviews in 2 that would attract the three speakers.

5 Work with a partner. Which of the adjectives you underlined in the texts in 2 might describe these services? Do you use services like these?

6 A ▶ 3.5 Listen to four people talking about a service from 5.
  1 Which service is each person talking about?
  2 How does the service make their life easier or what does it allow them to do?

7 Work with a partner. Make sentences using the words in this table.

Example:
Search engines allow people to find relevant websites.

Search engines	help	me	infinitive (with *to*)
Telecommunication	allow	you	
Financial advisers	make it easier for	companies	
Call centres		organizations	
Consultants	let	people	verb (without *to*)
Legal services		the world	

8 Work with a partner. Look back to the list you made for 1. Can you add any more services to it? They might be financial, travel, legal, or medical. Tell your partner about the benefits of these services.

Example:
My financial adviser helps me to plan my future.
Booking tickets online is really efficient and more cost-effective than using a travel agent.

3G TALKING ABOUT CHANGES

1 The pictures show some security measures. What are the advantages and disadvantages of each?

2 A ▶ 3.6 Listen to two extracts from a meeting.
1 What are the current and new security systems?
2 What are the good and bad points of the new system?

3 A ▶ 3.6 Match 1–10 to a–j. Then listen again and check your answers.
1 What I want to do today, … ____
2 I'll talk about … ____
3 As you know, we've recently … ____
4 Up to now, … ____
5 As a result, … ____
6 What's the reason for … ____
7 It's because Security … ____
8 Can you tell us … ____
9 Do you mean that … ____
10 The current situation, as it stands, … ____

a more about them?
b changing the current system?
c no one has stolen anything …
d been having a few problems …
e is to explain …
f the background to the situation …
g we have to swipe every time …?
h can't always check …
i simply doesn't prevent …
j we've been installing …

4 Put the phrases in **3** into these categories.
a Introduce a talk
b Give background information
c Ask for information / clarification / an explanation
d Give an explanation / reason

5 Work with a partner. Read your emails below, make notes on them, and then take turns to give an update. Listen to your partner's update and ask for an explanation. Listen again, and then ask for further clarification.

Student A

As many of you are aware, we've recently been having a number of problems with the underground car park. In one case, an employee had her bag stolen from her car. As a result, we've decided to install CCTV in all parts of the car park and in the corridors around the offices.

By the end of the month, you will see these cameras around the building. The cameras are connected to TV screens at reception.

Student B

As many of you know, we've recently had a number of problems with virus programs on the network. In one case, a hacker tried to read private employee information.

As a result, we've decided to install a new software program and to start a new system of passwords by the end of the month. The new software will automatically scan your computer when you open it. You will also receive a new password every month to log on to your computer. Your department manager will give you this password on the 1st of every month. Please do not pass this on to anyone else.

6 Work with a partner or in small groups. Think of a situation at work / school that changed, either recently or in the past. Explain the original circumstances, what the change was, and the reasons for it. Be prepared to answer any questions. It might be:
- a new security system
- a reorganization of your working space
- a reorganization of your class structure
- a new pricing system
- a new delivery system
- a change in your way of travelling to work / school.

3H PRESENTING PLANS

1 Do you have fixed working hours or does your company let you work flexitime?

2 What are the advantages and disadvantages of fixed hours and flexitime?

3 **V▶3** Watch the video. Paul, an HR manager, is giving an informal presentation during a meeting with his team. Make notes about the presentation's three main points.

Background

The three-part process

Core hours

4 **V▶3** Watch the video again. Match the beginnings 1–9 and endings a–i of each phrase.

1 As you know _____
2 We are going to _____
3 This is a _____
4 The MD would like _____
5 What we have is _____
6 How are we going _____
7 As you can see, _____
8 I'm dealing with _____
9 Can I ask you to _____

a take a look at these lists?
b that issue under 'What?' and 'How?'
c be implementing flexible working hours wherever possible.
d a three-part process.
e to implement all these changes?
f I've listed all the departments and teams into three groups.
g huge change to our company culture
h we are relocating.
i someone to look into the whole process ...

5 Your MD has asked each of you to think about a change to be made to the company. This could be anything from a change in the working hours to getting new drinks machines. Plan to give a short presentation about this.

6 Think of a change and make some notes on why the change needs to be made. In the DVD, Paul used 'Who?', 'What?', 'How?' to introduce his change. Look back at 3 for help on how to structure your presentation and look at 4 for useful language. Make notes but do not write down everything you want to say. Work with a partner and give your presentation. Your partner should give you feedback on what was good and how to improve.

7 After you have practised in pairs, form a group of four or five. Give your presentation to the group. As you listen to the other presentations, ask the speaker questions if you want clarification or further information.

4A DESCRIBING GRAPHS

1 Complete these graphs.

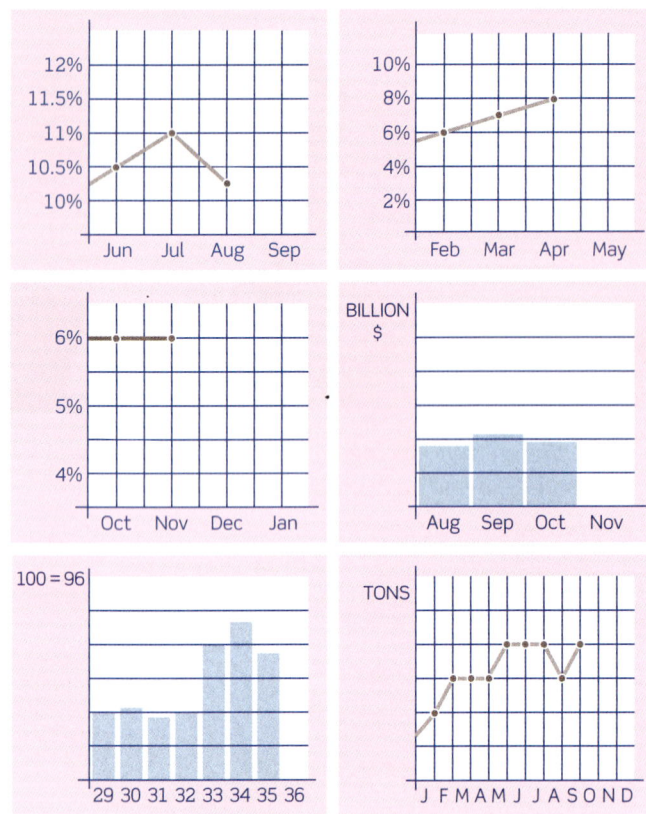

1 The rate of unemployment increased to 11% in September.
2 Interest rates decreased by 2% in May.
3 Inflation went down from 5.5% in December to 5% in January.
4 Consumer spending rose sharply in November.
5 The retail price index went up slightly in week 36.
6 Production fell steadily in the last quarter of the year.

2 [A ▶ 4.1] Listen to a sales manager describing her company's sales figures and complete this graph.

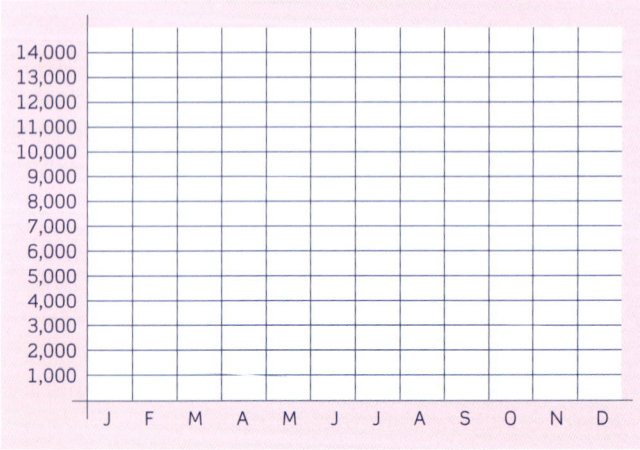

3 [A ▶ 4.1] Listen again and say why these things happened.
1 Sales increased in March.
2 Sales fell in May.
3 Sales rose in July.
4 Sales increased in September.
5 Sales went down in November.

4 Complete these sentences about the sales figures. Use a preposition (*to, from, by, at,* etc.).
1 Sales stayed _____ 6,000 in February.
2 They rose _____ 7,000 in March _____ 8,000 in April.
3 They decreased _____ 3,000 in May.
4 They fell _____ 4,000 in June.
5 They increased _____ 5,000 _____ 6,000 in August.
6 They increased _____ 7,000 between August and October.
7 They remained steady _____ 7,000 in December.

5 Mark the points on the graph by following the descriptions of sales performance.

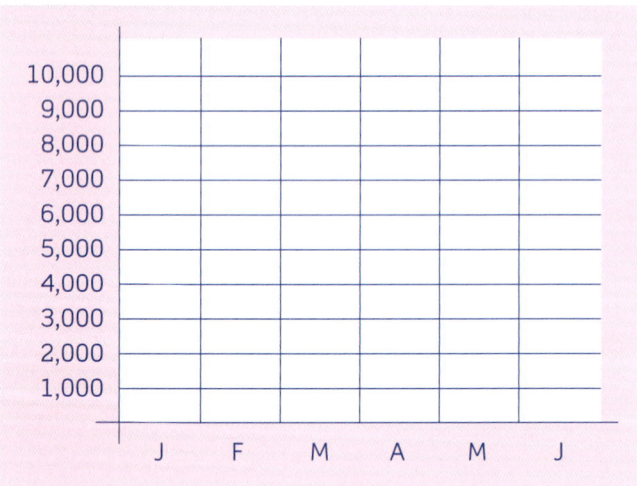

January: started the year at 9,000
February: fell by 5,000
March: rose to 7,000
April: decreased by 1,000
May: remained steady
June: dropped to 4,000

6 Now make your own graph. Describe it to your partner. Your partner must draw a new graph from your description. At the end, compare your graphs.

4B DESCRIBING CHANGES

1 Discuss these figures with a partner. One person should use the information in the left-hand column and the other should use the information in the right-hand column. Use these verbs.

↑ increase, rise, go up, jump
↓ decrease, fall, go down, drop

Example:
A Our market share fell by 1% last year.
B Yes, but on the other hand, our turnover increased by 8%.

Our gross revenues +8%	Our market share −1%
Prices of raw materials −4%	Distribution costs +18%
Spending on research and development +9%	The number of new contracts −6%
Debts to our suppliers −4%	Earnings from investments −3%
Productivity +6%	The number of employees −4%
Sales to South America +5%	Sales to the EU −2%
Our staff turnover −20%	Salaries +8%
Customer complaints −16%	Spending on training +15%

2 Which parts of the table do these sentences describe?
  1 There was a dramatic increase in this.
  2 This decreased slightly.
  3 There was a sharp rise in this.

3 Complete this table.

Adjective (describes a noun)	Adverb (describes a verb)
slight	slightly
sharp	
dramatic	
steady	

4 Which adjective / adverb describes:
  1 a sudden, very large change? _____
  2 a sudden, large change? _____
  3 a very small change? _____
  4 a gradual change (not sudden)? _____

5 Use each adverb and adjective once to complete this description.

Sales in the U.S. rose ¹_____ between 2007 and 2009. There was a ²_____ decrease in 2010 when our main distributor went out of business. Sales rose ³_____ in 2011, and the ⁴_____ improvement in 2012 brought us back to the 2007 level. There was a ⁵_____ rise in exports in 2008. They went up ⁶_____ in 2009 when we began to break into the Chinese market. They rose ⁷_____ in 2010 when we signed the new distributor agreements and there was a ⁸_____ increase in 2011 and 2012.

6 Think about an aspect of your company, school, or country where there have been changes over the last year or two. Draw a bar chart for the last 12 months – one bar per month.

7 Now work with a partner and describe your bar chart to your partner using the adjectives and adverbs on this page. Your partner must draw a new graph from your description. At the end, compare your graphs.

4 GRAPHS & TABLES

4C COMPARING VISUAL INFORMATION

1 Look at these statistics on sales of frozen foods. Which one is:
 1 a bar graph?
 2 a table?
 3 a pie chart?

a

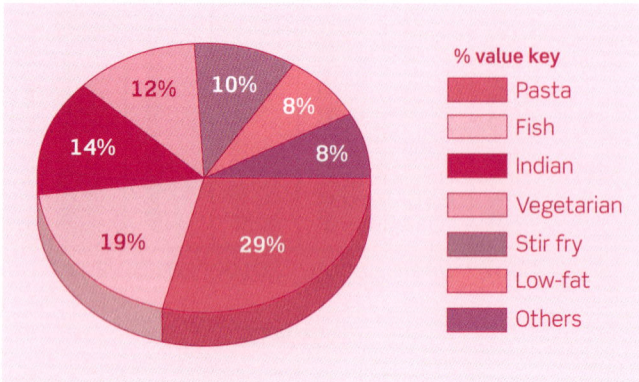

b

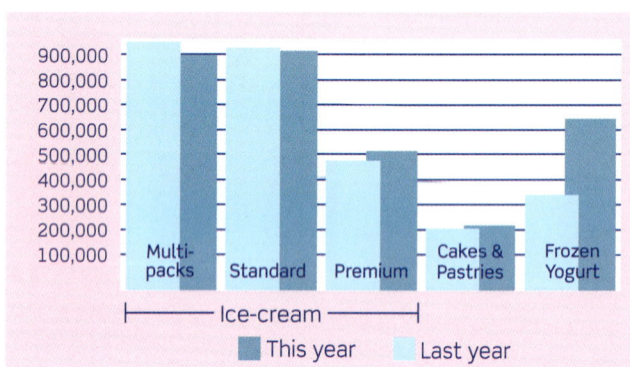

c

	Value ($000)	Volume (tons)
Meat and poultry	20,000	7,690
Vegetables	9,200	8,120
Fish	6,000	1,410
Ready meals	5,300	1,170
Desserts	2,600	770
Pizzas	2,300	330
Fruit	100	40
Totals	45,500	19,530

2 Match these headings to the correct graph, table, or chart in **1**.
 1 Desserts – sales by value _____
 2 Ready meals – sales by sector _____
 3 Frozen foods – sales by sector _____

3 [A ▶ 4.2, 4.3, 4.4] Listen to some retailers discussing the figures. You will hear three parts of their conversation. Match each part to the correct statistics.

4 [A ▶ 4.2] Listen to the first conversation again. Are these statements true (T) or false (F)? Correct the ones that are false.
 1 Sales are lower than last year. _____
 2 Multi-pack and standard sales are higher. _____
 3 Margins are better on premium brands. _____
 4 Yogurts have low margins. _____

5 [A ▶ 4.3] Listen to the second conversation again.
 1 Why are meat and poultry sales falling?
 2 What's the fastest-growing product line?

6 [A ▶ 4.4] Listen to the third conversation again. Complete the missing words.
 1 A Yes. We're offering a _____, and consumers are becoming _____. About half our sales are international recipes now.
 2 B And curries?
    A Yes, spicy dishes like curries are doing well. But the market's becoming _____, and some prices have come down.

7 Three companies produce the cardboard boxes you need. You are deciding which company to buy from. Your purchasing department has collected these statistics to help you make up your mind. Work with a partner and discuss which supplier is the best and why.

	EGP	The Card Company	Paper Packs Inc.
Price per standard 1 cubic metre box	7.56	7.4	7.83
No. of styles of boxes in the range	27	16	25
Quality – faults per 1,000 units	0.1	1.3	2.5
Delivery period	2 days	1 day	4 days
Discount	5%	10%	15%
Quantity kept in stock	100,000	600,000	500,000
Terms of payment	14 days	30 days	60 days

4D EXPLAINING CAUSE AND EFFECT

1 Look at the figures below. In which month did events 1–6 happen?

Milwaukee Branch

Overheads	July $	Aug $	Sept $	Oct $	Nov $	Dec $
Rent	690	950	950	950	950	950
Gas and electricity charges	560	560	600	1,300	700	900
Postage costs	600	610	1,500	590	630	580
Travel costs	250	400	320	2,800	590	280
Telephone charges	460	490	280	280	290	270
Entertainment costs	640	520	500	490	2,100	650

1 a direct mailing _____
2 a spell of cold weather _____
3 a move to a larger building _____
4 the installation of an Internet-based phone system
  _____
5 the launch party for the new season's designs
  _____
6 the annual sales conference in Cancún
  _____

2 Work with a partner. Ask and answer questions about the figures.

Example:
A Why was there an increase in rent in August?
B That was because of a move to a larger building.

3 Write sentences explaining the figures.

A move to a larger building (Reason)	resulted in	an increase in rent in August. (Result)
	led to	
The increase in rent in August (Result)	was the result of	a move to a larger building. (Reason)
	was due to	

4 Study the sentences below. Which are reasons and which are results? Link them with one of the phrases above.

1 The factory automation _____ an increase in productivity.
2 The staff reductions _____ the factory automation.
3 The large pay rise _____ a decrease in staff turnover.
4 The cost savings _____ the new ERP system.
5 The big orders from Japan _____ a recovery in sales.
6 The shorter delivery times _____ the new distribution system.
7 The increase in competition _____ a decrease in our market share.
8 The higher distribution costs _____ the increase in gas prices.

5 Draw a graph representing something connected with the world of work, for example:
- seasonal sales trends
- annual revenues
- material prices
- number of employees

6 Work with a partner or in small groups. Take turns presenting your graphs to one another.
- Explain what they represent.
- Give reasons for the changes.
- Answer questions.

These phrases will help you.

This graph shows …
As you can see …
This led to …
This resulted in …
This was due to …
This was the result of …
Are there any questions?

4E INTERPRETING FINANCIAL RESULTS

1 Graphic Images has just published its annual profit and loss account. Match these explanations to the correct items from the table below.
   1 money paid to the stockholders _____
   2 the cost of delivering goods to the customers _____
   3 the money kept in the company and added to the reserves _____
   4 the cost of managing the company _____
   5 the cost of raw materials and manufacturing _____

GRAPHIC IMAGES INC.
Consolidated Profit and Loss Account

	This year ($m)	Last year ($m)
Domestic sales	189	175
Export sales	181	191
Gross revenues	370	366
Cost of goods sold	(254)	(255)
Gross margin	116	111
Distribution costs	(17)	(17)
General administrative costs	(35)	(30)
Net income before tax	64	64
Tax	(23)	(22)
Net income after tax	41	42
Dividend	(36)	(34)
Retained earnings	5	8

2 Work with a partner. Ask and answer questions about the figures in 1.
   A What's happened to sales this year?
   B They've increased / gone up / risen.
   A What about net income after tax?
   B It's decreased / gone down / fallen.

3 Study these regional sales results. Which regions:
   1 have met their target?
   2 have exceeded their target?
   3 haven't met their target?

Region	Last year	This year	Target	Difference (%)
Northeast	4,200	5,250	6,000	-12.5
West	5,400	7,300	7,000	+4.3
Mid-Atlantic	4,110	5,500	5,500	0
Midwest	2,950	4,250	4,000	+6.25
Southwest	2,950	4,600	4,600	0
Southeast	4,100	5,650	5,800	-2.6

4 Work with a partner. Ask and answer questions about the figures.
   A How many units did they sell in the northeast last year?
   B They sold 4,200.
   A And how many have they sold this year?
   B They've sold 5,250. They haven't met their target.

5 You work for a pharmaceutical company. Your sales team sells two drugs: Mevacin and Rovocor. You want to give a prize to your best salesperson. Work with a partner. Student A looks at table A, below, and Student B looks at table B.

Student A: Ask questions and complete the table. Then decide who this year's 'top salesperson' is.

Student B: Ask questions and complete the table. Then decide who this year's 'top salesperson' is.

Table A (Eastern Region) Sales Results

		Last year	This year	Target	Difference
Catherine Ceretta	Mevacin	2,900	4,100	4,250	-3.6%
	Rovocor				
Hyojung Gye	Mevacin	4,850	6,150	6,000	+2.5%
	Rovocor				
Peter Vogel	Mevacin	3,950	3,900	5,000	-22%
	Rovocor				

Table B (Eastern Region) Sales Results

		Last year	This year	Target	Difference
Catherine Ceretta	Mevacin				
	Rovocor	3,400	4,600	4,000	+15%
Hyojung Gye	Mevacin				
	Rovocor	3,050	3,500	4,000	-12.5%
Peter Vogel	Mevacin				
	Rovocor	3,150	5,250	4,000	+31.25%

4F REPORTING ON SALES FIGURES

1 When you have good news to report, how do you prefer to report it? By email, at a presentation, one-to-one? What about bad news? Discuss with a partner.

2 How do you prefer to receive good or bad news?

3 [A ▶ 4.5] Listen to part of a meeting.
  1 What is the meeting about?
  2 What time of the year is the meeting taking place?
  3 Is Mike pleased with the results for his department? Why?

4 [A ▶ 4.5] Now listen again and complete the table with the missing information for home sales.

HOME SALES (TARGET INCREASE = 12.5%)

	Jan/Mar	Apr/Jun	Jul/Sep	Oct/Dec*	Total*
Compared to last year			+9.2%		+8%*
Units sold	(6,550)	(6,830)	(6,250)		(26,680)*

*forecasted results / sales

5 [A ▶ 4.6] Now listen to the Export Sales Manager's report. Complete the table with the missing information for export sales.

EXPORT SALES (TARGET INCREASE = 7.5%)

	Jan/Mar	Apr/Jun	Jul/Sep	Oct/Dec*	Total*
Compared to last year	+8.8%			+13.5%	
Units sold	(7,250)	(8,750)	(9,250)		(32,750)*

*forecasted results / sales

6 [A ▶ 4.6] Now listen again. Complete these sentences with the words she uses.
  1 Well, _____ that the export market is doing really well.
  2 I'm delighted to tell you that we have been able to sell _____ 9,000 units for the first time in the department, a _____ which represents an increase of 11.4%.
  3 The forecast for the final quarter is also _____.
  4 Obviously, _____ about the way the department has been working this year.
  5 We have _____ in eastern Europe and the new Madrid office has increased its sales by just over 20% since January, which is _____.

7 Report on developments in ABC Ltd for this year. Use the table below and try to use the same language that Tony and Susan used above.

8 You are the manager of ABC Ltd. Write a short report about the ABC results.

ABC LTD TARGETS FOR PRESENT YEAR

CONCEPT	LAST YEAR	THIS YEAR	TARGET
Sales	$23m	$25.5m	$24m
Profit margin	8.4%	9.7%	9.5%
Productivity	81%	89%	90%
Units sold	31,500	37,350	35,500
Employee satisfaction	78%	89%	85%
Client satisfaction	83%	95%	95%
Number of new clients	165	236	235
Average delivery time	24 days	21 days	22 days

4 GRAPHS & TABLES

33

4G DESCRIBING A PROCESS

1 Work with a partner. Brainstorm the stages for any of the following processes.
   - applying for a job
   - moving office
   - buying a house

2 Compare your stages with another pair. Who has the most stages? Are they all necessary?

3 Read this company information and answer these questions.
   1 What kind of fuel do you use in your car? How is biodiesel different?
   2 Is the oil from the jatropha plant a recent discovery?

D1 OILS: BUILDING ITS BIODIESEL BUSINESS

D1 Oils is a UK-based global producer of biodiesel. It designs, builds, owns, operates, and markets biodiesel refineries. Its vision is to be the world's leading biodiesel business.

Each refinery can produce 8,000 tonnes of biodiesel per year from vegetable oils, including jatropha.

The jatropha plant originated in South America, where its leaves and seeds were used as medicines. It has also been used for centuries to make oil lamps.

4 [A ▶ 4.7] A biofuels company wants to open a new refinery. The CEO, Dr Karl Kirstler, is explaining the process to potential investors. Listen and answer these questions.
   1 Is the basic procedure complex or simple?
   2 What are the main stages of the process?
   3 What is the end product?

5 [A ▶ 4.7] Listen again and complete sentences 1–6.

1 _____ the biodiesel fuel _____ the jatropha plant.
2 Trucks _____ the seeds.
3 _____ them (the seeds) _____ a grinder.
4 Oil is _____ of the seeds.
5 _____ it and _____ it with methanol.
6 _____ it _____ any transport vehicle.

6 Work with a partner. Look at this process of recycling printer ink cartridges. Which verb phrases in 5 can you use to describe the actions in stages 1–4?

Example: Take the cartridge out of the printer.

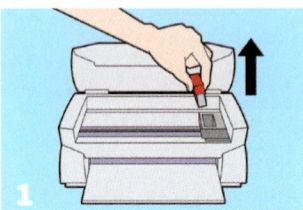 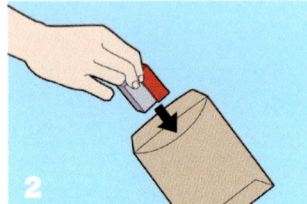
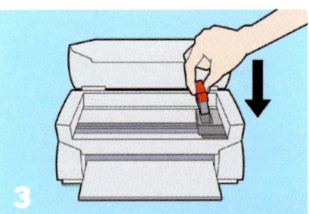 

7 These phrases are from the audio extract in question 4. Put them in the order (1–6) you would use them to describe the process in 6.
   a Once ..., you're ready to ... ___
   b The basic procedure is ... ___
   c Essentially, there are ... main stages. ___
   d First of all, ... ___
   e Having done / finished / brought, etc. ..., you ... ___
   f Finally, ... ___

8 Choose one of these processes and list the main stages using the phrases from 7.
   - loading new software onto a computer
   - preparing for a business trip
   - going through an airport – from arriving at the entrance to getting on the plane

9 Work with a partner. Take turns to describe your processes from 8. Does your partner think you included every stage?

10 Work with a partner. Prepare a visual aid to show the stages of a process you are very familiar with. Then present the process to the rest of the class.

4H USING VISUALS IN A PRESENTATION

1 Work in groups of four and discuss these questions.
   1 When you give a presentation, what kinds of visual aids do you normally use?
   2 How important are visual aids in your presentations? Are they always necessary?

2 **V▶4** Watch the video. Patricia Reyes, a market researcher, is presenting the results of a survey. During her presentation, she uses five different types of visual aids. Number them in the order she uses them (1–5).
   a a handout with the findings of the survey _____
   b slides with bullet points showing the key points _____
   c bar charts with scales from 1-10 _____
   d a pie chart showing responses from three regions _____
   e a flow chart showing the research process _____

3 **V▶4** Watch the video again and answer the questions below about the visual aids she uses.

Extract 1: PowerPoint slides
1 Write down the three words on her first slide.
2 What were the two key questions the survey needed to answer?

Extract 2: flow charts, pie charts, and handouts
3 Patricia's third slide shows a flow chart describing the survey. 90,000 customers were selected. What percentage responded?
4 What does the blue section in the pie chart represent?

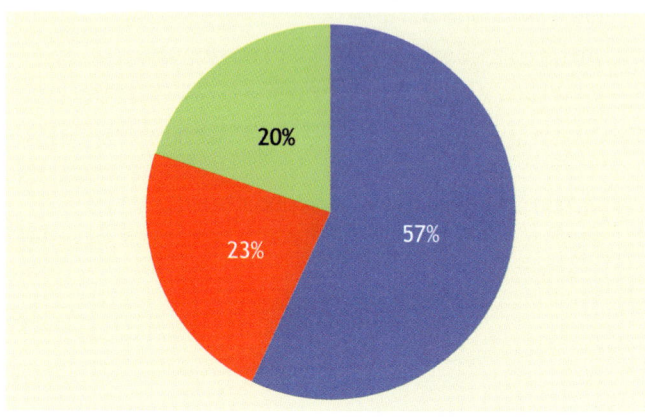

Extract 3: bar charts

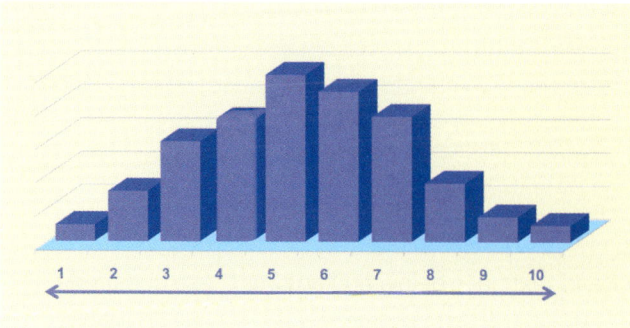

5 The first bar chart has a scale along the bottom from 1-10. What do these numbers represent?
6 Does the chart suggest that customers would recommend QPG?
7 In her second bar chart, what do the red and yellow bars represent?

4 Complete this extract from Patricia's presentation by replacing the words in *italics* with one of the verbs below. In some cases, more than one answer is possible.

break down into   summarize   illustrate   indicate

> I'm going to *sum up* [1]_____ the key findings … According to this chart the overall response *suggests* [2]_____ that customers are fairly likely to recommend your company. However, this chart *represents* [3]_____ the average response across the three regions. If we *divide* these responses *into* [4]_____ the three regions like this, it *shows* [5]_____ the difference in customer satisfaction region by region.

5 Work on your own. You are going to prepare a short presentation describing your typical working life. If you don't have a job, imagine one you'd like to do. Draw three simple visual aids that show the following information:
   1 The basic management structure of your department (or company).
   2 A flow chart showing a process you follow in your daily work.
   3 A pie chart showing (in percentages) how your working day (or week) is divided. You can decide on the categories, e.g. the time you spend in meetings, working alone, and travelling.

6 Work in groups. Give a short presentation about your working life using your visual aids from 5.

7 After the presentations, discuss which visual aids were effective and why.

BUSINESS WRITING 5

5A INTRODUCTION TO EMAILS, LETTERS, AND MEMOS

1 Look at these situations and decide if you would write an email, letter, or memo for them.
   1 You want to invite a colleague to lunch.
   2 You need to tell your department about an important meeting they should attend.
   3 You want to apply for a job.
   4 You want to make a complaint about some poor service you have received.

2 Read texts a–c below and answer these questions.
   1 Match the texts to the following types of business writing.
      memo _____
      email _____
      letter _____
   2 Who do you think is the sender and who is the receiver in each text (e.g. boss, client, supplier, colleague, employees)?

a
Hi
We're having the meeting Tuesday! Hope you can come. Sorry about the short notice.
Thanks.
All the best
Joel

b
Dear Mr Owen
I am writing to introduce myself. I am your new sales contact for Taylor and Whitaker and I look forward to working with you in the future. I will be in your area next week and would like the opportunity to meet you.

Please do not hesitate to contact me about this or any other matter in the future. I am always available on 0970 567 4738.
Yours sincerely
Nile Peterson

c
To: All staff
From: FD
Subject: Meet our Spanish sales office colleagues
Remember the meeting on Tuesday at 10.00 a.m. Our Spanish sales team is here for the day so please attend.

3 Work with a partner and discuss the following questions.
   1 What types of business writing do you do (in your own language and in English)?
   2 Who do you write to?
   3 Who do you get emails, memos, or letters from?

4 Read the texts again. Then work with a partner and match texts a–c to sentences 1–9. Sometimes, more than one answer is possible.
   1 The sender knows the receiver very well. _____
   2 More than one person received this. _____
   3 The sender doesn't know the receiver very well. _____
   4 It is formal and very polite. _____
   5 It is friendly. _____
   6 It is very direct and not very friendly. _____
   7 The sender wants a reply or further contact. _____
   8 The sender doesn't expect a reply. _____
   9 The sender wants to arrange a meeting. _____

5 Read these rules for writing a memo. Choose the correct option from the words in *italics*.
   Rules for writing memos:
   1 Write who it is to and from at the *beginning / end* of the memo.
   2 *Do / Don't* write a subject line.
   3 Try to write about *two or three subjects / one subject* in each memo.
   4 *Do / Don't* use short and clear sentences.
   5 Be *informal / direct* and polite.

6 Work with a partner. Write rules for one of the following, then compare your rules with another pair.
   1 writing informal emails
   2 writing formal business letters

   Think about the following:
   • Starting and ending   • Structure
   • Being polite   • Being clear

7 Write one of the following. Remember to follow your rules from 5 and 6.
   1 An email to a colleague – ask to meet tomorrow. Say when and where.
   2 A letter to introduce yourself to a new customer – request a meeting.
   3 A memo to everyone in your department – you want them to meet an important visitor next week. Say when and where.

5B STRUCTURING A LETTER

1 When did you last write a letter (or email):
- asking for information?
- giving information?
- saying sorry?
- saying thank you?
- accepting an invitation?
- congratulating someone?

Who was it to? What was the result?

2 Read this letter and answer the questions.
1 What kind of letter is it?
2 What did the writer and recipient do yesterday?
3 What extra information does the writer give?

a 45 Dale Road
Stevenage
SG6 6SB
UK

Sandman Creek Summer Camps b
1831 Ellis Avenue
Eugene OR 97405

25 November, 20__ c

Dear Mr Hemingway d

I am writing to thank you for the interview we had yesterday. I am very interested in working in your summer camp next year. I hope that my qualifications and interests were suitable. I meant to also mention that I am learning to drive and I hope to have my driving licence before the summer. e

Once again, thank you for seeing me. I look forward to hearing from you. f

Yours sincerely g

Amanda Nash h
Amanda Nash i

3 Match parts a–i in the letter to these sections.
1 opening salutation ____
2 closing sentence ____
3 full name (typed) ____
4 closing salutation ____
5 writer's address ____
6 signature ____
7 date ____
8 body ____
9 recipient's address ____

4 What are the differences in structure between a letter and an email? Does the letter in 2 follow the rules of letter writing in your country?

5 Look at these opening and closing salutations. Can you think of any other ways to open and close a letter?

Dear Mr ...
Dear Ms ...
Yours sincerely

6 Lay out the content of this letter correctly on a computer or rewrite it on a piece of paper.

128 Springfield Drive, Seattle, WA 98199

Raglan Business Solutions, 860 Lincoln House, Spokane, WA 99201

5 March, 20—Dear Ms Moran I am writing to thank you for your offer of an internship in June. I am very excited by the opportunity of working in your company.

I look forward to receiving your information pack.

Yours sincerely

Irene Porter
Irene Porter

5C WRITING A COMPLAINT

1 Look at the picture. What has happened?

2 Have you ever had to complain about something you bought? What did you buy? What did you do about it?

3 Read the letter extract below. Which sections fulfil these functions?
1 Detailing the problem.
2 Additional relevant information.
3 The effect the problem had on the customer.
4 Request for action.

Dear Sir or Madam

On the 28th of February I ordered a pair of jeans (size XS) from you. Confirmation came immediately, but when your package arrived today it was a pair of jeans in size XXL. There seems to have been some confusion with another order. In addition, you appear to have charged me €49.99, instead of the advertised price of €29.99. This has made me overdrawn at the bank and I now risk getting bank charges. Please send the correct jeans as soon as possible, and reimburse me the amount you owe me. Meanwhile, what shall I do with the other pair?

Yours

Jane Harris

Jane Harris

---

4 Find expressions from the letter which match the meanings below.
1 you said you could supply it _____
2 what caused the problem _____
3 another problem is _____
4 I think your bill is wrong _____
5 this is what I want you to do _____
6 tell me what to do _____

5 Look at these sentences from a letter of complaint. Which ones are polite (P) and which ones are impolite (I)?
1 You made a mistake. _____
2 There seems to be a mistake. _____
3 You appear to have charged me too much. _____
4 And another thing … _____
5 Your bill was wrong. _____
6 What are you going to do about it? _____
7 Please rectify this mistake at the earliest possible opportunity. _____
8 I would be grateful if you could … _____

6 Discuss with a partner. Is it better to complain politely or impolitely?

7 A group of students has done a summer course at a university. What four things do they complain about?

Dear Ms Hay

We booked 25 places on the Coral University summer school Economics course, which we recently attended. The bill has just arrived, ¹_____ in it. You have overcharged us, because your bill is for AU $87,500, ²_____ for the course, because we have already paid a deposit of $875 per person. In addition, the course was 175 hours long, instead of 200, so there should be ³_____ 12.5%. ⁴_____ a corrected bill. Meanwhile, we would like you to know that the facilities ⁵_____. Firstly, the classrooms seemed to have no air conditioning and they were poor quality. Secondly, they were a long way from the main campus facilities. All in all, we are dissatisfied with the ⁶_____ that the university provided.

Yours sincerely

Yaxi

---

8 Complete the email in **7** with the words used for complaining below.
a were not of a very high standard
b a reduction of
c Please send us
d which is not the correct price
e but I am afraid there is a mistake
f standard of service

9 Work with a partner. Think of a recent occasion when you received poor service or the wrong product. Write a letter of complaint about it.

5D RESPONDING TO A COMPLAINT

1 Read this letter of complaint quickly. Find out what the problem is and what the person wants done. Is the letter polite?

> Dear Sir or Madam
>
> I am writing to complain about the recent order we placed with your company. Unfortunately, the order was not supplied correctly, so I am writing to ask for an explanation as to what happened and how it will be remedied.
>
> On 30th October this year, we placed an order with your company for 10,000 items. However, on taking delivery of the shipment, it was discovered that you had sent only 8,000 units but had invoiced us for 10,000.
>
> This shortfall has put our company in a difficult position, as we were due to supply one of our major customers and as such we were unable to fulfil their order.
>
> Please could you look into what happened and obviously make up the shortfall in our order immediately. While we do not wish this incident to have a long-term effect on our working relationship, we will be forced to take further action if the problem is not resolved at the earliest opportunity.
>
> I look forward to hearing from you shortly.
>
> Yours faithfully
>
> *Chris Vidic*
>
> Chris Vidic

2 Work with a partner and discuss how you would respond to the complaint.

3 Work with a partner and decide which of the following is good advice when responding to a complaint.
1 Explain how the trouble occurred
2 Express sincere regret.
3 Blame the customer.
4 Tell the customer they are the only person who complained.
5 Explain what you intend to do to rectify the situation.
6 Make promises you can't keep.
7 Trivialize the complaint – 'this is no big deal'.
8 Offer a goodwill gesture.
9 Promise to get to the bottom of the problem.

4 In what order would you put the steps you chose in **3** in a letter of response to a complaint?

5 Look at expressions 1–6 below. Match each one to a piece of good advice in **3**. Then match 1–6 to a–f below to construct a letter responding to the complaint in **1**.
1 I'm terribly sorry to hear about _____
2 I'm afraid we have been having _____
3 I will be investigating what exactly happened _____
4 In the meantime, I've arranged for _____
5 We would like to offer you _____
6 Once again, please accept our sincere apologies _____

a ... a 10% discount off your next order as we value your custom greatly.
b ... problems with our inventory system recently.
c ... the problems you've had with this shipment.
d ... for the inconvenience this has caused you.
e ... to make sure this problem doesn't occur again.
f ... the outstanding 2,000 units to be dispatched to you today.

6 Match a–f below to a phrase with a similar meaning from 1–6 in **5** above.
a What I'll do immediately is to get ...
b I would like to apologize for ...
c I hope you will accept ...
d I'm afraid this was because of ...
e I really do apologize for ...
f I would like to look into this further

7 Choose one of the problems below and write a letter of complaint.
- A new computer has broken down after just two days.
- You have just received a delivery where all the goods were damaged.
- You have just come back from a business trip and your baggage was lost.

8 When you have finished, swap letters with a partner and respond to the letter of complaint that you have received as sympathetically as possible. Use the information in **4**, **5**, and **6** to help you.

5E PLACING AN ORDER

1 Discuss these questions with a partner.
1 What sort of things would an office need to order?
2 What information do you need to give when you order products?

2 Complete the email with these words:

order   confirmation   arrange   send
agreed   conversation   check

Dear Mr Price

Following our telephone ¹_____ this morning we would like to place an ²_____ for the following six printers:

   3 x model number CGW560
   3 x model number DJ360

Could you ³_____ delivery by the end of the month? Please ⁴_____ the items to:

   Coffee Beans Premier Inc.
   Unit 4
   Thornhill Business Estate
   Oxford
   OX6 TBG

We would like to ⁵_____ that the prices are as stated in your catalogue, with a 15% discount as ⁶_____ with you on the phone.

As before, we will pay by credit card on receipt of invoice.

We look forward to your ⁷_____ of this order.

Yours sincerely

Emily Buchanan

Facilities Department

---

3 Read the email and answer these questions.
1 Has Emily spoken to Mr Price?
2 What did they agree on the phone?
3 Does Emily have any requirements about delivery?
4 How is she going to pay?

4 Work with a partner. You have been asked to order some new office furniture. Before writing to a supplier, discuss what you could ask them about the order.

5 Now read this email. Compare it to your ideas in **4**.

Dear Sir or Madam

I am **looking into** purchasing a new range of office furniture for my company. I have looked at your online catalogue and have found a number of items that would **suit our needs**.

Before I place an order, though, I would like to ask if you can offer us a **discount** for a **bulk order**. We need to buy 110 desks, 125 office chairs, and 35 storage cabinets. There is a possibility of **future purchases** of similar items.

We would need delivery of all items **by the end of** next month. We are in the south-west of Scotland.

I look forward to hearing from you.

Yours

Emma Sandford

Carters Investments

---

6 Match the words in **bold** in the email in **5** to these equivalent phrases.
1 meet our requirements _____
2 trying to find out about _____
3 at or before _____
4 money off _____
5 a large order _____
6 further orders _____

7 You are in charge of office supplies at a company called Sportdirect. Write an email ordering a selection of the items from the catalogue below. You can spend around £25.00. This is the first time you have made contact with the office suppliers.

HIGHLIGHTERS	
Wallet of 4	£2.50
Wallet of 8	£4.50

SELF-STICK NOTES	
Pack of 10 (38mm x 51mm)	£6.50
Pack of 10 (76mm x 76mm)	£11.90

ROLLERBALL PENS	
Pack of 12	£10.90

TRANSPARENT OFFICE TAPE	
12 rolls of small core tape	£6.50
12 rolls of large core tape	£8.50

5F CONFIRMING AN ORDER

1 Work with a partner and discuss the following questions.
  1 Have you ever ordered one thing and received another?
  2 Why do you think that orders sometimes go wrong?

2 Read the email confirming an order and answer the following questions.
  1 What has been ordered?
  2 How many have been ordered?
  3 How much will it cost?
  4 When will it be shipped?

Dear Mr Adams

1 Thank you for your order. Your purchase information **appears** below. Please take a moment to read through this email and **check** that the order details are correct.

2 You have placed an order for 25 of our new OP245Y laptops. The cost, after **discount**, is 900 euros per laptop. The total cost of the order is 22,500 euros. This is the amount we will **issue** an **invoice** for.

3 You will be pleased to know that we have the laptops **in stock** and can have them ready to be shipped within 24 hours of you confirming your order.

4 If you are happy with all these **details**, please send me an email to confirm the order and we will **process** it straightaway.

Best regards

Nemone Skolska

---

3 Read the email again and decide if these statements are true (T) or false (F).
  1 Nemone is writing to confirm the details of the order. ____
  2 Mr Adams's company will pay full price for the goods. ____
  3 Some of the laptops are out of stock. ____
  4 Mr Adams has to reply to this email. ____

4 Match paragraphs 1–4 in the email to functions a–d.
  a Invite a response. ____
  b Introduce the reason for writing. ____
  c Confirm details. ____
  d Give information / news. ____

5 Read the following paragraph. Which paragraph in the email could it replace? How would the other paragraphs need to change if you used this alternative paragraph?

> Unfortunately, the model you have ordered is currently out of stock. We are expecting a delivery in five days, but if you prefer we could send you the OP245Z model which we have in stock now.

6 Match the words in **bold** in the email to definitions 1–8.
  1 a reduction in the usual price ____
  2 facts / information about something ____
  3 be present / be noticeable ____
  4 when a shop / factory has something available for sale / use ____
  5 an official list of items or work done plus the cost ____
  6 to deal with something in an official way ____
  7 to produce / provide something official ____
  8 to make certain that something is correct ____

7 Look at the order form and the notes made about it. Use the information to plan an email to Mr Noble. Decide what information you will give in each section of your email.

ORDER FORM

Date: 15.1.2012
Name: Ross Noble
Company: Gilbert's Engineering
Quantity: 30
Item: OP250YZ laptops
Price per item: 1,100 euros
Total Price: 33,000 euros

Regular customer

Quantity over 20 = discount 10% per unit (total price 29,700 euros)

Only 25 in stock, but we do have OP250S in stock.

8 Write the email to Mr Noble, then exchange emails with a partner. Give feedback on your partner's email.

5 BUSINESS WRITING

5G RESPONDING TO AN ENQUIRY

1 Look at this response to a letter of enquiry. How well do Tony and Claude know each other? How do you know?

AEK Software Plc
Berlin

Tony Fuchs
Promotech
The Sidlings
Aylesbury
H026 1VF

6 February, 2012

Re: Enquiry about the new operating system

Dear Mr Fuchs

Thank you for your letter dated 29.01 asking about our new operating systems. As you know from our previous communications, the new system will be launched in May this year.

The purpose of the system is to make day-to-day use quicker and more intuitive. In other words, we want the user to have everything at their fingertips. The new system is significantly different from the one that is currently in use.

As you point out, one downside is the need for initial training. The good news is that, as part of an introductory offer, all purchasers of the new operating system will be offered a free on-site training day with one of our developers.

You might be interested to know that there will be a preview of the system at an open day at our offices in April.

Please find enclosed the latest information leaflets, as you requested, and an invitation to the open day mentioned above. If you have any further questions, please do not hesitate to contact me.

Yours sincerely

Claude Fischer

Claude Fischer
Sales and Marketing Manager

---

2 What information does the letter not include? Tick [✔] or cross [✘] each piece of information below.
1 Information about availability of the product ____
2 Prices and delivery details ____
3 Details of a special offer ____
4 Details of a promotional event ____
5 A general description of the product ____

3 From the information contained in the reply, what do you think the original letter of enquiry said? Do you think this is a positive response? Why? / Why not?

4 Match these words and phrases from the text with definitions 1–5.

intuitive   at their fingertips   significantly
downsides   hesitate

1 ready and easy to use _____
2 the disadvantages or negative aspects
   _____
3 to pause before you do something _____
4 ability to know something by using feelings not facts
   _____
5 in a way that is large enough to be important
   _____

5 What is the purpose of each of the five paragraphs in the letter?

6 Underline words or phrases in the letter that help the writer to do these things.
1 Welcome the enquiry.
2 Acknowledge points in the original enquiry.
3 Try to avoid using the first person; *I* or *me*.
4 Refer to something that has already been talked about.
5 Introduce solutions.
6 Introduce a special offer / invitation.
7 Mention enclosures / attachments.
8 Invite further contact.

7 Read the short letter of enquiry below and highlight the areas that you would need to address when you are replying to it.

Dear Sir or Madam

I was recently sent a password and username for your Internet banking website, however, I have managed to lose it. Would it be possible for you to send the password again or will I have to re-register at the local branch?

Also, once I have access to the website will I be able to set up regular cash transfers overseas online?

Thank you for your prompt response.

Yours

Candace Park

---

8 Reply to the letter above. Make sure you answer the questions and give reasons. Also, take the opportunity to introduce a special offer to the customer.

5H WRITING AND RESPONDING TO INVITATIONS

1 When was the last time you were invited to a business or social event? What was it? How were you invited? Did you go?

2 Read the letter and answer the following questions.
1 When is the conference?
2 What is it about?
3 Who is the opening speaker?
4 When will Ingrid receive the full programme?
5 Why is Robert going to send the programme?
6 What do they want Ingrid to do?

Angel Life Organization
Piccadilly
London

Ingrid Marna
Executive Director
The Hope Foundation
Helgeandsholmen
Stockholm
7 April, 2012

Dear Ingrid

¹_____ our telephone conversation last week, this letter serves to formally invite you to the second International Ethical Business Conference.

The conference is to be held from April 4th–7th at the Keyworth Centre, part of London South Bank University. ²_____ you would be one of the keynote speakers at the event.

The theme of the conference is 'Ethical Business in the 21st Century' and we are planning an event for approximately 1,000 delegates. ³_____ Hal Gaur will be opening the event with a thought-provoking talk entitled 'It's the end of the (third) world as we know it', which examines how corruption and greed has led to an increased neglect of business ethics in developing countries.

⁴_____ give the final keynote speech. ⁵_____ base it on your recent research or, if you prefer, you are welcome to base it on other aspects in your area of specialism. We would be happy to discuss the content with you. We have invited several other distinguished speakers from the business and academic worlds and we will forward a complete speaker programme, with contact details, to you in a couple of weeks so that you get an idea of the specific subjects that will be covered by the other speakers.

To summarize, the Angel Life Organization would be pleased if you would agree to be our closing speaker at this year's conference. ⁶_____ your reply.

Yours sincerely

Robert Yates
Robert Yates

3 Complete the letter with phrases a–f.
a We wondered if you would like to
b Further to
c We look forward to
d We would be delighted if
e We would like you to
f We are pleased to announce that

4 Put the sentences in the correct order in Ingrid's reply to Robert's invitation.
a Please could you send me more details of the travel and accommodation arrangements? ___
b It sounds like a wonderful opportunity. ___
c Thank you very much for the invitation to speak at the IEB Conference this year. ___
d I look forward to hearing from you. ___
e If this is acceptable, I would be honoured to deliver the closing speech at the conference. ___
f I wondered if I could arrive on the 6th as I have other commitments that week. ___

5 Work with a partner. What would you say if:
1 you wanted more information before you accepted?
2 you had to reject the invitation?

6 Work with a partner and look at the letter in **2** again. What is the function of each paragraph?

7 Look at the details below. Write a letter to the main speaker asking him / her to come to the conference. Remember to organize your letter like the one in **2**.

> **Memo – Human Resource Management in 21th Century Conference**
>
> **Speaker:** J. Parker
>
> **Date of Conference:** 31st October – 3rd November
> **Date of Speech:** 31st October (opening plenary)
> **Title of Speech:** Speaker to choose own title
>
> **Other Speakers:** Tern Albract (closing plenary)
> Jana Smit (talk – title undecided)
> Meals and accommodation provided.

8 Once you have finished, swap your letter with someone else in the class. Write a response to the invitation you receive.

5 BUSINESS WRITING

6 JOB APPLICATIONS

6A JOB ADS AND DESCRIPTIONS

1 Have you ever looked for a job? What are the main things you look at when reading job adverts?

2 Read these three job ads and answer the questions.
   1 Which ad is for a part-time post?
   2 What do all three ads want the candidates to have?
   3 Which job offers training?
   4 Which ad has requirements for how the candidate should look?
   5 Which ads state a perk that the successful candidate will get?
   6 Which ads state the exact hours that the successful candidate will be working?

Trainee retail manager for 24-hour supermarket
Hours: 35 hours per week on a shift basis
Salary: £18,000 per annum + bonus
Description: Applicants should preferably have some experience in retail and be aged 18–25. No higher education qualifications are necessary as training is given. The job will involve cash handling, stock control, supervising staff, and dealing with customer complaints. Applicants must be prepared to work some night shifts. Possibilities for career development in the company.

BAR STAFF
Are you a student? Do you need to make money while you study? Why not join the staff at the Riverside Café-Bar?
Hours: 20 hours per week (part-time)
Wages: £140 per week
Must have experience of working in the food and drink industry, and have a friendly manner and smart appearance. Applicants must be aged 18+. Applicants can choose their preferred working times.

Salesperson
Hours: Monday to Friday, 8.30 a.m. to 5.30 p.m.
Wages: £15 per hour
The perfect job for someone who wants to progress in the world of sales and marketing. Applicants must have some previous experience within a sales environment. You will be required to generate new business and you must have a valid, clean driving licence as a company car will be provided.

3 Match the phrases from the ads to their definitions.
   1 Should preferably have some experience in ____
   2 The job will involve ____
   3 Possibilities for career development ____
   4 Must have experience of ____
   5 You will be required to ____

   a It is essential to have experience in
   b The tasks of the job include
   c The job could lead to more senior posts
   d It is useful to have experience in
   e The employee will have to

4 Alexis Gourrier has decided he needs to find a job that he can do at the same time as he studies at school. Read the notes he has made.

- born in Paris, 21 years old
- baccalauréat, two years ago. 13 out of 20
- finishing first year of 2-year course in sales and marketing at technical college in Rennes
- speak good English and basic German
- can use several word-processing packages
- last year was a group leader at summer camp in the USA
- summer before worked at Big Burgers serving customers
- before starting sales and marketing course worked in a printing shop, producing business cards, etc. for 2 months
- play the drums, swimming, diving
- would like something with training / promotion prospects
- shift work OK, but prefer normal hours – need time to do work for course though

5 Work in groups of two or three and discuss which job you think would suit Alexis the best and why. Try to agree on one job.

6 Write a job ad for your ideal job.

6B WRITING A CV

1 What is a curriculum vitae (CV)? Do you have an up-to-date one? What information is on it?

2 **A ▶ 6.1** Listen to a personnel officer talking about the dos and don'ts of writing CVs. Make notes on the following points. Do you agree with what she says?

Topic	Do	Don't
Personal details		
Education		
Qualifications		
Work experience		
Photographs		

3 These are headings and categories commonly used in CVs.

marital status   referees   employment history
permanent address   educational history   skills
title   personal details   hobbies and interests
surname   qualifications   date of birth

Which one means:

1 basic facts about you? _____
2 practical abilities? _____
3 where you live most of the time? _____
4 what you do in your free time? _____
5 when you were born? _____
6 Mr, Mrs, Ms, or Dr? _____
7 details about your working life? _____
8 whether you are married or single? _____
9 people who can tell the employer about your qualities and character? _____
10 proof that you have successfully completed a course? _____
11 schools and colleges? _____
12 family name? _____

4 Which information is not usually asked for in your country? Should you give any information that is not mentioned here?

5 Read the CV. Complete a–h with appropriate headings or categories from the list in 3.

Toni Carter

a _____
Full name: Toni (Antonella) Carter
b _____: 14/02/78
Permanent address: Linden Cottage, 88 Whitecross Road, Rickmansworth, Herts, WD3 8KY
Tel: 01923 0845841
Mobile: 07897 765782
Personal email: CarterToni@gratisserve.co.uk

c _____
I am currently following a part-time MBA programme in international business at Randolph Business School.
1997–2000: University of Nottingham
    BSc Business Studies (2:1).
1994–1996: Dr Chalmer's Sixth Form College
    A-levels in Italian (A), Mathematics (B), Biology (B).

d _____
Word-processing. Excel. PowerPoint.
Languages: Bilingual (English / Italian).

e _____
September 2002–present
    Farinelli Fashions: Marketing Executive with responsibility for customer services. I regularly visit sales outlets in the south of England and our suppliers' factories in Malta and Morocco.
January 2001–September 2002
    Kilt Corner: Shop Assistant, then Deputy Manager.
August–December 2000
    La Sorpresa Italian Restaurant: Part-time Waitress.

f _____
Football: At university I was captain of the women's football team.
Playing the cello: Member of SN Chamber Orchestra.
Travel: In my gap year, I travelled round Australia and South East Asia. I developed a broader awareness of other cultures.

g _____

Catriona Flynn   Professor K. Pradesh
Manager, Kilt Corner   Randolph Business School
Gorton Street   32 City Road
London, W8 7AT   London, EC1A 7HG

6 Read the CV again and answer these questions.

1 Does Toni follow all the advice?
2 What details does she give of her personal achievements?
3 What does she hope to prove by giving details of her interests and hobbies?

7 Create your own CV using Toni's as a guide.

6C WRITING A COVERING LETTER

1 A CV or job application form should always be accompanied by a short covering letter. What is the purpose of a covering letter?

2 Read this advice about writing covering letters. Does the same apply in your country? Discuss with a partner.
- Always type a covering letter unless you are specifically asked for a handwritten one.
- Where possible, address it to the person concerned.
- Keep it short – use only one side of a page.
- Make sure that the page isn't too full and that the layout is clear.

3 Read the covering letter below and answer these questions.
1 What job do you think the writer is applying for?
2 What kind of organization does he want to work for?
3 How well does he 'sell' himself?

Dear Mrs Proctor

I am writing in response to your advertisement in the September edition of *Telemarketing Magazine* and would like to be considered for one of the Trainee Consultant posts mentioned.

As you will see from my enclosed CV, I have recently completed a degree in international marketing at Clifton University. A six-month company placement in France gave me the opportunity to put some of the theory learned on my course into practice, and to acquire a good working knowledge of French. The post involved helping with the development of telemarketing scripts for salespeople. Since then, I have had several months' experience of working in the international section of the Automobile Club's call centre. This means I have had direct experience of the day-to-day realities of communicating with the public.

From your corporate website, it appears that working for your organization would offer a stimulating and challenging career within a highly competitive field. I am extremely attracted by this opportunity and feel that I have already acquired some of the skills and awareness necessary to make an effective contribution to the company.

I am currently available for interview and would welcome the opportunity to discuss the post in more detail. I look forward to hearing from you.

Yours sincerely

Russell Fleming

Russell Fleming

4 The letter is divided into four paragraphs. In which paragraph (1–4) does he:
a state his enthusiasm and interest? _____
b say when he could be interviewed? _____
c show that he knows something about the organization he wants to work for? _____
d say how he heard about the job and state his interest in it? _____
e describe his practical work experience? _____
f include details of relevant skills? _____

5 The language in Russell's letter is formal. Put the words and phrases below into the correct part of the table – formal or informal.

~~begin~~   at the moment   complete   reply
please find enclosed   free   answer   available
another thing   ~~commence~~   request   in addition
available jobs   give you   ask for   discuss
vacancies   currently   I have included   talk about
job   provide you with   post   finish

Formal	Informal
commence	begin

6 Using Russell's letter as a guide, write a covering letter in reply to one of the job advertisements on page 44. Include some of the formal words and expressions in **5** (up to eight) but avoid making your letter sound too formal.

7 Swap your letter with a partner and work together to try to improve each other's letters.

6D VIDEO CVS

1 Have you ever made or seen a video CV? What makes it different from a written CV? Would you use it in the same way as a written CV?

2 **V▶5** Watch the video. Take notes about the different filming techniques for the CVs. Discuss your notes with a partner. Which technique did you prefer? Why?

3 **V▶5** Watch the video again. Complete the notes about each candidate in the table.

	Dacia	Yang	Adam	Bryony
Personal details				Doesn't say
Education, training, and qualifications				
Other skills	Doesn't say	Doesn't say		
Work experience				
Interests and hobbies				Doesn't say

4 Complete these phrases from the video using a word from the list. Then watch the video again or read the transcript and check your answers.

training   major   received   attended
interacting   self   practical   undergoing

1 I'm an electrical engineer by _____.
2 I've _____ a BSc in electrical and computer engineering.
3 I did my undergraduate degree at University of Newcastle upon Tyne, and my _____ was in economics.
4 I have been _____-employed all of my working life.
5 I have learnt pretty much all of my experience from _____ application.
6 I've _____ a Harvard Business School executive education course.
7 I'm _____ my MBA at Cranfield.
8 I enjoy _____ with people.

5 In groups, discuss these questions about the video CVs. Give reasons for your answers.
   1 Which candidates communicated effectively in the video? How?
   2 How could you improve some of the video CVs?

6 Work with a partner. Discuss and write a list of general advice for people making a video CV. Afterwards, compare your list with the rest of the class.

7 Write a script for your own video CV. Decide if you want it to be in the form of an interview or a monologue. If you have a video recorder, record your video CV and then show it to the class. If you don't have a video recorder, simply give your video CV to the class as if to a camera.

8 As a group, discuss and analyse everyone's video CVs. Offer advice on how they could be improved.

9 Based on the advice you received from your classmates, re-write your video CV and repeat steps **7** and **8** above.

6E IDENTIFYING YOUR STRENGTHS AND SKILLS

1 Why is it a good idea to know what your strengths and weaknesses are?

2 Complete the instructions on this form to try to identify your skills and strengths.

KNOW YOURSELF

1 Write five adjectives which describe your personality.

- _____
- _____
- _____
- _____
- _____

2 Circle four skill areas below that reflect your skills most closely.

3 Then, for each skill area you circled, choose and circle a key area that best reflects your strengths. You will now have four circled skill areas and four circled key areas.

TRANSFERABLE SKILLS

SKILL AREAS	KEY AREAS
Creative	generate new ideas imaginative able to find solutions
Collecting information	good at research can analyse information can write reports can work with systems
Organization	good at planning meet deadlines good at time management
Communication	make presentations listen well speak clearly good at languages

SKILL AREAS	KEY AREAS
People skills	work in teams handle conflict help people advise people
Entrepreneurial	innovative positive thinker take risks determined
Self-management	self-motivated able to make decisions willing to learn solve problems have attention to detail
Information technology	word processing, graphics, databases, email/Internet, spreadsheets, PowerPoint

3 Think about a personal example for each key area that you circled. Make notes. Be ready to discuss this with a partner.

Skill area: Creative
Key area: Imaginative
Personal example: I designed the cover for my sister's demo CD.

4 Work with a partner. Discuss your answers with your partner. Ask your partner questions about their personal examples. Discuss what type of job or career you are suited to.

5 Share your discussion with the class. Make a class list of the different career / job areas you are each suited to. How varied is the list?

6F PREPARING FOR AN INTERVIEW

1 Read the article below and match some of the interview mistakes with this advice.
  a Don't wear the wrong clothes.
  b Don't eat or drink.
  c Do your homework – learn about the company.
  d Prepare appropriate answers to questions.
  e Don't appear tired or bored.
  f Don't keep checking the time.

How NOT to impress at an interview!

Going for a job interview is a chance to impress and show a company your best qualities. Or it should be! Interviewers told us about their worst experiences. Are you ready for some surprises?

1 One woman started eating a hamburger and fries during the interview. She said that she hadn't had lunch.

2 One candidate saw a photo of my wife on the desk and asked if it was my mother.

3 I was amazed when a woman brought her dog to the interview. She even asked for a bowl of water.

4 I must be very boring. A candidate once went to sleep during the interview. I had to wake him up!

5 The candidate made a phone call on his mobile. It was to his brother – he asked him how to answer the question.

6 During the interview, an alarm clock went off in the candidate's bag. He got up and said he had to leave because he had another interview.

7 Our company does telemarketing. But one candidate said she didn't like talking on the phone!

8 A candidate came in wearing earphones. She said she could listen to me and to the music at the same time.

9 We interviewed someone who forgot the name of our company halfway through the interview. We weren't impressed.

10 Our company has a casual dress policy. But one candidate took this too far! He came to the interview wearing shorts, flip-flops, and a T-shirt.

2 Work in groups. Decide which candidate's behaviour was:
  1 the most embarrassing
  2 the most stupid
  3 the most offensive
  4 the most inappropriate.

3 Work with a partner. Imagine you are interviewing someone to be the secretary of your place of study. What questions would you ask?

4 Interviewers want to know about your education and past experience, what sort of person you are, and what you can offer. Read the key questions below.

Write your answers to these questions.

Key interview questions
1 What were your best / worst subjects at school?
2 What skills and qualities do you have?
3 What are some of your strengths and weaknesses?
4 Tell me about an achievement in your last job or at school.
5 Why are you interested in this company?
6 What experience have you had of working in a team or a group?

5 Work with a partner. Ask and answer the questions in 4.

6 JOB APPLICATIONS

49

6G GOING TO A JOB INTERVIEW (1)

1 Work with a partner. Make a list of ways you could improve your chances of success in a job interview.

2 Read the advice below about going to a job interview. What does it say about the following areas?

1	Research	
2	Attitude	
3	Skills and qualities	
4	Questions	

The perfect interviewee

As the person applying for the job, you need to do your research before the interview. Check the company's website, read recent news about the company, and talk to people who know the company. During the interview, try to demonstrate you have done your research as it shows you are serious about the position.

Most interviews have similar questions. Think carefully about what questions you will be asked and prepare positive answers in advance. Be clear about what strengths, skills, and qualities you want them to notice in you, especially ones that are relevant to the job. If you need to discuss any challenges or weaknesses, then explain how you intend to overcome them. In general, try to present a positive version of yourself. Dress well, try to relax, maintain eye contact, and be friendly and enthusiastic.

Finally, prepare questions which you would like to ask. Remember that good questions will demonstrate that you have done your research and have thought carefully about the requirements of the job.

3 ▶6 Monica has applied for the position of Finance Assistant in the Finance Department of QPG. Watch her job interview with Paul (Head of HR) and Maja (Head of Finance) and make notes on this form about her.

Name: _Monica Bagley_
Current job: [1] _____
Reason(s) for applying:
[2] _____

Employment history:
Worked for the accountants Reynolds and Waters.
Duties included: [3] _____
Reason for leaving previous job:
[4] _____
Relevant skills for this position:
[5] _____
Candidate's expectations of the position
(e.g. challenges of the post):
[6] _____
Reason why the candidate thinks he / she would be suitable:
[7] _____
Possible training this candidate may require:
[8] _____
Action needed: _Email Monica details of_
[9] _____

4 ▶6 Watch Monica's job interview again and analyse her performance. Rate each item below using the following scale:

1 = successful 2 = satisfactory 3 = unsuccessful

Appearance _____
Demonstrates research _____
Gives positive answers with examples _____
Has prepared answers to common questions _____
Asks her own relevant questions _____
Gives a good impression _____

5 Discuss, in small groups, how Monica could have improved her performance in the interview. Where did she go wrong? Could she be better prepared? Share your ideas with the class. Decide if you would offer her the job.

6H GOING TO A JOB INTERVIEW (2)

1 How many job interviews have you had? Talk about them in small groups. What were the interviews like? How did you perform? Did you get the job(s)?

2 During an interview, you will need to talk about your personal qualities. Look at these job advert extracts. Underline the adjectives that are used to describe personal qualities. Discuss with a partner what they mean.

> **AMBITIOUS, HARD-WORKING INDIVIDUALS NEEDED FOR SALES POSITIONS!**
> Are you an intelligent, resourceful, and outgoing person looking to start a successful career in sales?

> **TRAINEE SOFTWARE DEVELOPER**
> Fantastic opportunity for an enthusiastic and creative individual to join our innovative software development team. You will have excellent IT skills, including experience of website design, and be passionate about gaming software.

3 Read these comments by candidates in interviews. Match the personal qualities to the comments.

ambitious   enthusiastic   reliable   flexible
decisive   determined   hard-working   creative

1 My last manager trusted me and let me deal with clients on my own.
2 I like to think that I always approach any new task with a positive attitude and a smile.
3 I'm able to make tough decisions when I have to.
4 I think it's important to achieve your aims and I always try my hardest to make sure this happens.
5 I suppose in two or three years' time I'd hope to see myself promoted to a senior position.
6 I'm able to work with most people and adapt to different working environments.
7 I don't mind working late or working extra hours when there's a lot of work to do.
8 I've been told that I'm pretty good at coming up with new ideas.

4 Work with a partner or in small groups. One person is a candidate who is applying for one of these posts. The other person (or people) works for the employer and is going to interview the candidate.

> **Telephone Banking Advisor**
> A major bank is seeking Customer Advisors to work in their call centre in Swansea, Wales. As an advisor you will be taking calls from banking customers and dealing with general customer queries. Along with providing excellent customer service, you will be expected to promote the bank's products and services. Call centre experience desirable but full training provided. Apply initially by sending your CV and a covering letter.

> **Area Sales Manager, southern Europe**
> Leading educational publisher is looking to recruit an Area Sales Manager for southern Europe. This is an exciting opportunity for an ambitious individual who is passionate about the university sector. Sales experience required along with the ability to speak Spanish and Italian. The post offers a competitive salary along with an annual bonus and a company car.

5 Spend some time preparing for the interview. The candidate chooses the post and thinks of possible answers to questions and of questions to ask. The interviewer(s) should think about what skills and qualities they are looking for in the candidate and prepare their questions.

6 When you are ready, start the interview. Afterwards, swap roles and practise another interview using the job in the other advert.

GRAMMAR FILES

PRESENT SIMPLE

FORM
Positive: Add *-s* or *-es* after the verb with *he / she / it*.
  I / you / we / they **specialize** *in Latin American music.*
  He / She / It **specializes** *in high-tech products.*

Negative: Use the auxiliary *do / does* + *not* + verb.
  It **doesn't** *produce software.*
  We **don't** *produce mobile phones.*

Questions
1 Use *do* and *does*, but don't change the form of the main verb (no -s).
  Does *it have a subsidiary in China?*
  Do *you have many competitors?*

2 With question words (*who, what, where, how*, etc.), use *do* and *does* after the question word.
  Where **do** *you work?*
  What **does** *he do?*

Exceptions
1 In questions with *be*, do not use *do* and *does*.
  Is he Spanish?
  Where are the subsidiaries?

2 In negative sentences with *be*, add *not* or *n't*.
  I'm **not** *from China.*
  They are **n't** *in the company today.*

USE
1 To talk about facts or things which are generally true.
  The company provides insurance services.

2 To talk about regular actions.
  We have sales meetings every month.

3 Do not use the Present Simple to talk about actions in progress at this moment. Use the Present Continuous for this.

1 Complete the sentences with a verb from the list.

start   starts   work   works   is
are   specialize   specializes   have   ~~has~~

1 The company _has_ three subsidiaries in the Far East.
2 She _____ in Manchester today.
3 We _____ in the advertising of children's toys.
4 The meeting always _____ at 2.30 p.m.
5 She _____ for an engineering company.
6 They usually _____ work at about 7 a.m.
7 I _____ one office in Paris and another in Buenos Aires.
8 He's a lawyer. He _____ in company law.
9 Most of our competitors _____ in Europe.
10 I _____ in sales.

2 Choose the correct answer from the words in *italics* to complete questions a–j. Then match a question to answers 1–10 in **1**.

a Where *has / does* the company have subsidiaries?
b Where *be / is* she?
c What sort of products *do / does* you specialize in?
d What time *do / does* the meeting start?
e Who *do / does* your wife work for?
f When do they *start / starts* work?
g *Have you / Do you have* an office in Paris?
h What *is / does* he do?
i Who *do be / are* your competitors?
j What *do / does* you do?

PRESENT CONTINUOUS

FORM
Positive: Use *am / is / are* + *-ing* form.
  He **'s preparing** *his presentation.*

Negative: Use *am / is / are* + *not* + *-ing* form.
  They **'re not going** *to the meeting.*

Questions: Put *am / is / are* before the subject.
  Are *you staying in this hotel?*
  Where **is** *she working?*

USE
1 To describe actions in progress at the moment of speaking.
  Hi. I'm calling you from my car.

2 To describe actions in progress around the present time, but not always at the moment of speaking.
  He's doing a very interesting course this month.

1 Match questions 1–6 with answers a–f.

1 What is she doing? _c_
2 What does she do? ____
3 Are you working this week? ____
4 Do you work at weekends? ____
5 Why do you leave the office so late? ____
6 Why are you leaving the office so late? ____

a She's a teacher.
b Yes, but only four days.
c ~~A master's in business studies.~~
d My boss always asks to see me at about 7 p.m.
e We had a very long meeting.
f No, never.

GRAMMAR FILES

2 Read this email and choose the correct form of the verb in *italics*.

> Hello
>
> I ¹*write / am writing* to ask if you ²*have / are having* a sales office or sales rep in Argentina. I ³*work / am working* for a small computer producer here and we ⁴*look / are looking* for a new supplier of sound cards. We usually ⁵*buy / are buying* from a supplier in the USA, but their products ⁶*become / are becoming* too expensive for us.
>
> We have over 30 shops in Argentina and we ⁷*open / are opening* another five this year. We also regularly ⁸*get / are getting* business by mail order via our website.
>
> We ⁹*try / are trying* to find a new supplier before the end of this month, so please contact me as soon as possible.
>
> Best regards
>
> Elena Suarez

QUESTIONS

FORM

1 The normal order of words in a question is question word or phrase + auxiliary + subject + verb.
> *Where do you work?*
> *How many days is he staying?*

2 The order of words is the same even when the subject consists of several words.
> *What time are the CEO and the Production Manager arriving?*

3 In questions with a *yes / no* answer, the order of words is auxiliary + subject + verb.
> *Does he work in production?*
> *Are you opening a new office?*

4 The auxiliary and verb form are different for each tense.
Present Simple: *do / does* + verb.
> *Where **does** he live?*

Present Continuous: *am / is / are* + *-ing*.
> *Why **are** you **calling**?*

Past Simple: *did* + verb.
> *What time **did** you arrive?*

Exceptions

1 When the verb *be* is the main verb, there is no auxiliary. The order of words in a question is question word(s) + verb + subject.
> *What time is the meeting?*
> *Where was he yesterday?*

2 When the question word (or words) is the subject of the sentence, there is no auxiliary. The order of words is question word(s) + verb.
> *Who works here?*
> *How many people are coming?*

1 Choose the correct question, a or b.

1. a Where does your boss work?
   b Where works your boss?
2. a What do you make products here?
   b What products do you make here?
3. a Why is changing your logo?
   b Why is your logo changing?
4. a Do you have a canteen here?
   b Have you a canteen here?
5. a How often the company does launch new products?
   b How often does the company launch new products?
6. a Who does the Sales Manager report to?
   b Who the Sales Manager reports to?
7. a Does the company opening any new factories?
   b Is the company opening any new factories?
8. a How long ago did you move here?
   b How long you did move here ago?
9. a When do your offices are open?
   b When are your offices open?
10. a How many people do work in this department?
    b How many people work in this department?

2 A manager of Wrigley's, famous for its chewing gum, is answering questions about the company. Look at his answers and decide what questions the journalist asked. Use the words in *italics* to help you and add any other words you need.

1. *your / Where / sell / products / you*
   Q <u>Where do you sell your products</u>?
   A In more than 150 countries.
2. *the company / when / start*
   Q _____?
   A In 1891.
3. *its head office / have / where / it*
   Q _____?
   A In Chicago.

GRAMMAR FILES

4 people / employ / many / the company / How
Q _____?
A About 15,000.

5 competitors / have / the USA / many / you
Q _____?
A Yes, we do. There are about 14 chewing gum producers in the States.

6 percentage / you / in the USA / market / have / of / What
Q _____?
A Around 60%.

7 chewing gum / much / Americans / How / eat
Q _____?
A The average American eats 180 servings of gum per year.

8 main customers / Who
Q _____?
A Young people in the 12–24 age group.

9 famous brands / the company / What / sell
Q _____?
A Orbit, Freedent, Extra, Eclipse ... and others too.

10 new products / develop / you
Q _____?
A Yes, we are. We're developing innovative new brands.

PAST SIMPLE

FORM

Positive

1 Add *-ed* to the infinitive of regular verbs.
   We **started** work at 7.00 yesterday.

2 Add *-d* to the infinitive or regular verbs ending in *-e*.
   She **lived** in Switzerland.

3 Change the *-y* to *-i* and add *-ed* to regular verbs ending in consonant + *-y*.
   He **tried** to find a new job.

4 Double the final consonant of short regular verbs ending in vowel + consonant.
   I **stopped** the car.

5 Many verbs are irregular. Irregular verb forms do not end in *-ed*.

Negative
Put *didn't* before the infinitive of both regular and irregular verbs.
   I **didn't** want to be late for the meeting.
   They **didn't** see the manager.

Questions
Put *did* before the subject and the infinitive of both regular and irregular verbs.
   When **did** they arrive?
   Where **did** you go?

USE

1 Use the Past Simple to describe a finished action in the past.
   They sent the parcel on Monday, but it didn't arrive until Friday.

2 Words and phrases we often use with the past simple are *yesterday, last week, last year, in 2005, five years ago*.

1 Complete the text with the Past Simple form of the verbs in brackets.

Last week, I ¹ _was_ (be) very busy. On Monday morning, our biggest customer ² _____ (visit) our factory. I ³ _____ (meet) her at the airport at 7.00 in the morning and ⁴ _____ (take) her to the plant. In the afternoon, we ⁵ _____ (have) a meeting which ⁶ _____ (not finish) late, but she ⁷ _____ (want) to see a show afterwards. On Tuesday, I ⁸ _____ (fly) to Berlin for a conference. In the afternoon, I ⁹ _____ (make) a presentation which ¹⁰ _____ (not go) very well. The next day, I ¹¹ _____ (go) to Stuttgart to meet a supplier. On Thursday, we ¹² _____ (interview) candidates for the new sales jobs, but we ¹³ _____ (not find) anybody suitable. In the evening, I ¹⁴ _____ (play) squash in the company tournament but, unfortunately, I ¹⁵ _____ (not win). On Friday, I ¹⁶ _____ (reply) to all my emails and ¹⁷ _____ (write) a proposal for an Austrian company. In the afternoon, I ¹⁸ _____ (attend) a planning meeting which ¹⁹ _____ (end) very late in the evening. I ²⁰ _____ (not get) home until midnight!

GRAMMAR FILES

2 Complete the questions.
1. _What time did they arrive_?
   They arrived at nine o'clock.
2. Where _____?
   We had lunch in the staff canteen.
3. Who _____ at the conference?
   I saw our colleagues from the Buenos Aires office.
4. Why _____ the meeting?
   The manager left the meeting because he had an urgent phone call.
5. Which hotel _____ at?
   They stayed at the Hilton.
6. When _____ join the company?
   She joined the company last year.
7. How long _____ with the visitors?
   I spent all day with them.
8. How many emails _____?
   We sent about a hundred.

PRESENT PERFECT

FORM
Positive: have / has + past participle form.
   I **have (I've) finished** my work.
   He **has (He's) written** three letters today.

Negative: have / has + not + past participle.
   They **haven't done** the work this week.
   The post **hasn't arrived** yet.

Questions: Put have / has before the subject.
   Have you seen the new Production Manager?
   Where **has** she been today?

USE
1. To talk about past actions where the time includes the present.
   I've made three presentations today / this week / this month.
2. To describe progress in a list of things to do, we use *already* and (*not*)... *yet*?
   Have you visited that customer **yet**?
   No, I haven't had time (**yet**). But I've **already** made an appointment with him.
3. To ask someone about general experiences in their life, we use *ever* or *never*.
   Have you **ever** seen the Taj Mahal?
   No, **never**.
4. Use the Present Perfect to talk about actions which started in the past and are continuing now.
   I've worked here for three years (and I still work here now).
5. For past actions where the time doesn't include the present, use the Past Simple.
   I haven't seen him today, but I saw him yesterday.

With *for* and *since*
1. To talk about an action that started in the past and is continuing now.
   I've worked for this company for ten years.
2. We use *for* with a period of time.
   She's had this job **for** a month / two years.
3. We use *since* with a precise date or point in time.
   They've been here **since** 2007 / August / this morning.

1 A customer service manager is talking about the situation in his department. Complete the text with the Present Perfect form of the verbs in brackets.

This month ¹_____ (hasn't been) a very good one for me. Three more members of my team ²_____ (tell) me that they are leaving the company. Two of them ³_____ (not / find) another job yet, but they say that the pressure of work ⁴_____ (become) too much for them. It's true that there ⁵_____ (be) a big increase in their workload this year because two other customer service assistants ⁶_____ (already / leave) the department and we ⁷_____ (not / recruit) anybody to replace them.
I ⁸_____ (ask) my boss several times if we can employ some new people for the team, but each time he ⁹_____ (say) that we need to reduce our salary costs. But I know we ¹⁰_____ (lose) some business because we ¹¹_____ (not / have) enough people to deal with customer calls.
The situation can't continue like this. I ¹²_____ (not / make) a final decision on this yet, but I'm thinking of leaving the company myself.

GRAMMAR FILES

2 Choose the correct answer from the words in *italics* to complete questions 1–8. Then match them with responses a–h.

1 *Did you read / Have you read* that article about e-recruitment last week?
2 *Did you see / Have you seen* the new Dalí exhibition yet?
3 *Have you ever / Did you yet* applied for a job online?
4 *Have you had / Did you have* any work experience when you joined this company?
5 *Has / Have* she made many calls today?
6 *Have / Did* all the candidates come for interview yesterday?
7 *Have you received / Did you receive* a bonus in the last six months?
8 *Have you learn / Did you learn* a lot in your last job?

a No, never. _____
b No, I haven't. Our results haven't been very good. _____
c Just one or two this morning. _____
d Yes, I did. I did several jobs when I was a student. _____
e No, I didn't. I didn't have much responsibility, so it was very boring. _____
f Yes, it was very well-written. _____
g Just one person wasn't there. _____
h No, I haven't had time. _____

3 Complete the sentences with *for* or *since*.

1 I have worked for the company *since* 1998.
2 I have been in my office _____ eight o'clock this morning.
3 We have been in this meeting _____ four hours!
4 I have known Keiko _____ we met at university.
5 I haven't read a good book _____ a long time.
6 I lived in Africa _____ four years before I moved to Thailand.
7 We need to increase sales. We haven't advertised _____ Christmas.
8 We have sold our products in Europe _____ January.

WILL / GOING TO / PRESENT CONTINUOUS

WILL

FORM

Positive: *will* + verb.
  I'll meet you at the reception desk in your hotel.

Negative: *won't* (*will not*) + verb.
  I won't disturb you.

Questions: *will* + subject + verb.
  Will you call me later?

USE

To make decisions at the moment of speaking.
  A *Can you let me have a number to contact you on?*
  B *Just a moment. I'll give you my business card.*

GOING TO

FORM

Positive: *am / is / are* + *going to* + verb.
  I'm going to look for a new job after the holidays.

Negative: *am / is / are* + *not* + *going to* + verb.
  He isn't going to work late tonight.

Questions: *am / is / are* + subject + *going to* + verb.
  Are they going to look for a new head of department?

USE

To talk about a plan that we have already decided.
  We're going to move to the new office in the spring.

PRESENT CONTINUOUS

FORM
See page 52.

USE

To talk about a future arrangement someone has made. The arrangement usually has a fixed time or place.
  A *What are you doing tomorrow after work?*
  B *I'm taking my daughter to the dentist.*

GRAMMAR FILES

1 Choose the correct answer from the words in *italics*.
  1 There's no message. *I'm calling / I'll call* back later this afternoon.
  2 It's her fiftieth birthday so *she's going to have / she'll have* a party.
  3 You can call at any time because we *aren't going / won't go* out.
  4 *I'm going to wash / I'll wash* my car tonight. It's really dirty.
  5 He can't meet us tomorrow because *he'll visit / he's visiting* a client.
  6 Don't worry about the taxi. It *won't be / it isn't being* late.
  7 I can't stand my job any longer, so *I'm going to / I'll* look for a new one.
  8 *She's playing / she'll play* tennis tonight so she can't go to the dinner.

2 Complete the mini dialogues. Use the *will*, *going to*, or the Present Continuous form of the verbs in brackets.
  1 A I can't hear you very well.
     B I'm sorry. I'll _speak_ (speak) up a little.
  2 A Most of our deliveries were late yesterday.
     B I know. We _____ (get) a lot of complaints from customers.
  3 A How are you getting on with that project?
     B We _____ (not finish) it on time.
  4 A When are you going to talk to your boss about your timetable?
     B I _____ (meet) her tomorrow afternoon.
  5 A When do we have to pay the invoice by?
     B I'm not sure. I _____ (ask) one of my colleagues.
  6 A What are you doing tomorrow at one o'clock?
     B I _____ (have) lunch with a customer.
  7 A Can you tell me when my order will arrive?
     B Just a moment. I _____ (check) with the driver.

PASSIVE FORMS

FORM
Verbs in sentences can either be active or passive.
The passive is formed with the verb *be* + past participle of the main verb.

Tense	Passive form
Present Simple	The photocopier **is serviced** once a year. Our offices **are cleaned** in the evening.
Past Simple	The meeting **was held** yesterday. The new computers **were installed** last week.

USE
1 When the person who does the action is unknown.
   The flowers are changed daily.
   (I don't know who changes them.)
2 When the person who does the action is unimportant.
   The hotel was built in the 19th century.
   (It isn't important who built it.)
3 When the person who does the action is too obvious to mention.
   The books were delivered this morning.
   (It's obvious a delivery company brought the books.)
4 When we want to say who does something in a passive sentence, we use the preposition *by*.
   The party was organized by the social committee.

1 Correct these sentences.
  1 Deliveries are make three times a week.
     Deliveries are made three times a week.
  2 The invoice sent yesterday.
     _____.
  3 Over a thousand guests was invited to the event.
     _____.
  4 The post collects at 10 a.m. every day.
     _____.
  5 The software is written for our own engineers.
     _____.
  6 The meeting was cancelling because of the strike.
     _____.

2 Rewrite these sentences in the passive form starting with the words given.
  1 They serve hot meals in the staff canteen.
     Hot meals _are served in the staff canteen._
  2 The HR department sent an email to all employees.
     An email _____.
  3 Someone stole the money during the night.
     The money _____.
  4 The heads of department informed the staff about the decision.
     The staff _____.
  5 We discuss salaries with employees individually.
     Salaries _____.
  6 He keeps the key to the safe in his desk.
     The key to the safe _____.

57

GRAMMAR FILES

FIRST CONDITIONAL

FORM
There are two parts to a sentence in the first conditional: the condition and the result.

Positive and negative
1 Use *if* + Present Simple for the condition and *will / won't* + infinitive for the result.
   If they invite me to the opera, I'll accept the invitation.
   If we book an expensive restaurant, we won't have any money for taxis.

2 The sentence may begin with the condition or the result. Put a comma to separate the two parts when the condition comes first.
   If I work late tonight, I'll miss the football.
   I'll miss the football if I work late tonight.

Questions
The result usually comes first in first conditional questions. Put *will* before the subject and the infinitive of the verb after.
   How will you get to Paris if you miss your plane?
   Will the staff go on strike if they don't get a pay rise?

USE
To talk about events that will probably happen in the future.
   If the manager resigns, people will be very upset.
   If we finish the project by Friday, we won't have to work at the weekend.

1 Choose the correct answer from the words in *italics*.
1 If they *won't plan / don't plan* the event carefully, they *go / 'll go* over their budget.
2 If the venue *is / will be* too small, we *don't book / won't book* it.
3 He *doesn't get / won't get* a good deal if he *'ll wait / waits* any longer.
4 If we *don't hold / won't hold* a corporate event this year, we *lose / 'll lose* some of our clients.
5 The manager *doesn't accept / won't accept* the invitation if she *won't like / doesn't like* the venue.
6 If we *'ll arrange / arrange* a trip to the Guggenheim, we *don't arrive / won't arrive* back at the hotel in time for dinner.
7 They *'ll cancel / cancel* the outdoor activities if it *rains / 'll rain* at the weekend.

2 Rewrite the sentences using the prompts.
1 if / the weather / be / bad / we / not go / sailing
   If the weather is bad, we won't go sailing.
2 if / the singer / be ill / they / cancel / the concert
   _____.
3 we / not go / to the show / if / it / finish / late
   _____.
4 how / they / travel / if / the airline / be / on strike
   _____?
5 he / call / the host company / if / he / not receive / an invitation
   _____.
6 what / you / do / if / it / snow / on the day
   _____?
7 if / she / not like / the food / she / order / something different
   _____.

SECOND CONDITIONAL

FORM
Positive
1 *If* + Past Simple, *would / might* + infinitive (without *to*).
   If they dropped their prices, we would (we'd) buy their products.

2 The word *if* can also appear in the second part of the sentence.
   We would (We'd) send them a catalogue if we had their address.

3 You can replace *would* with *might*. In this case *might* means *perhaps*.
   If they offered me the job, I would accept it.
   (I'm sure I would accept it.)
   If they offered me the job, I might accept it.
   (Perhaps I would accept it.)

Negative
If + Past Simple negative, *would not* (*wouldn't*) + infinitive.
   If he didn't love city life, he wouldn't live there.

USE
1 To talk about things which will probably not happen and the results of these things.
   If there was a new job in New York, I'd apply for it.
   (But there probably won't be a job available.)

58

GRAMMAR FILES

2 To talk about impossible or hypothetical situations and their results.

If oil didn't exist, we wouldn't have all these pollution problems.

3 The second conditional is different from the first conditional.

First conditional: *If I have time, I'll call you.*
(It's possible or probable that I'll have time.)

Second conditional: *If I had time, I'd call you.*
(But I probably won't have time.)

Note that the past simple in a second conditional sentence refers to the present or the future. It doesn't refer to the past.

If they offered me the chance to work abroad (now / next year), I'd accept it.

1 Look at this book review and complete 1–9 with phrases a–i.

> What would you do if you were 50 years old and ¹ *you lost your job* ? If you ² _____ where your next pay cheque was coming from, ³ _____ setting up your own business? Journalist Matthew Colbert talked to 20 successful entrepreneurs who started their own companies after being made redundant in their fifties. He asked them what advice ⁴ _____ to people if they ⁵ _____ in the same situation. If ⁶ _____ their businesses again, ⁷ _____ things differently?
>
> **20 Lives That Began at 50** is a fascinating collection of interviews for anybody over 50 who's thought of starting their own company. If you ⁸ _____ one business book this year, this is the one ⁹ _____.

a might they do
b could only read
c they would give
d would you think about
e we would recommend
f they could start
g didn't know
h ~~you lost your job~~
i found themselves

2 Choose the correct answer from the words in *italics*.
1 I *would / will* travel around the world if I *has / had* enough money.
2 What part of your job *do / would* you delegate if you *had / would have* an assistant to help you?
3 If you *were / would be* me, *were / would* you sign the contract?
4 If we *would give / gave* them more money, they *worked / might work* during their holiday.
5 We *would finish / finished* on time if the electrician *worked / would work* faster.
6 *Would / Did* we receive the goods tomorrow if you *sent / would send* them today?
7 He *wouldn't / didn't* work late if you *wouldn't pay / didn't pay* him so well.

MODALS FOR ADVICE

MUST, MUSTN'T, SHOULD, SHOULDN'T, AND COULD + INFINITIVE

USE

These modals are used to give advice.

1 Use *must* or *mustn't* for something that is very important or necessary.

*You look ill. You **must** see a doctor.*
*You **mustn't** tell my boss I have a new job.*
(It's very important you don't tell him.)

2 Use *should* or *shouldn't* for something that is or isn't a good idea.

*You **should** stop smoking.*
(It would be a good idea.)

*You **shouldn't** drink alcohol at lunchtime.*
(It's not a good idea to do this.)

3 Use *could* for something that is a possible solution, but maybe not the best.

*You **could** speak to your boss about the problem.*

GRAMMAR FILES

FORM

Positive

There is no change in the form of modal verbs.

I / You / He / She / We / They must make a decision soon.

Negative

Add *-n't* to the verb. There is no *don't* or *doesn't*.

*You **mustn't** do that.*
(not *You don't must.*)

*He **shouldn't** call so late in the evening.*
(not *He doesn't should.*)

Questions

1 Modal verb + subject + verb.
   Should I accept that new job?
   Could I ask him to come later?

2 But when we ask for advice, we often prefer to begin the question with *Do you think ...?*
   Do you think I should accept that job?
   Do you think I could ask him to come later?

1 Match problems 1–7 to the advice a–g and choose the correct modal verb in *italics*.

1 Our competitor's new product is cheaper than ours. ____
2 Our salary costs are too high. ____
3 The new job is less interesting and it pays less. ____
4 Our restaurant is losing customers. ____
5 They've asked me to work in the international division. ____
6 I'm stressed at work. ____
7 I've made a big mistake in the accounts. ____

a You *should / shouldn't* ask for language lessons.
b You *could / mustn't* change the menus.
c You *could / mustn't* work such long hours.
d You *mustn't / must* recalculate your figures.
e I *think / don't think* you should accept it.
f You *shouldn't / could* reduce your price for the first three months.
g You *should / shouldn't* recruit any more people.

2 Aleksander is giving Natalia advice about writing a good CV. Three of the verbs in *italics* are correct, but five are incorrect. Find the five incorrect verbs and correct them.

Dear Natalia

You asked for help with writing your CV. Here are some ideas to help you.

Obviously, you ¹ *should* _____ forget your contact details (address, phone, etc.) and you ² *must* _____ include your education, work experience, and skills. You ³ *must* _____ include a photograph if you want, but it's not absolutely necessary.

It's a good idea to write quite a short CV, so you ⁴ *must* _____ write more than two pages, and don't forget, you ⁵ *should* _____ start with your most recent job first.

I think you ⁶ *should* _____ also write short sentences and use verbs with impact, for example, 'achieved my goals', 'improved my performance'.

Finally, you ⁷ *shouldn't* _____ check that you haven't made any spelling or grammar mistakes – and most importantly – you ⁸ *could* _____ always tell the truth!

Hope this is useful.

Best wishes

Aleksander

GRAMMAR FILES

MODALS FOR OBLIGATION

USE

1 To describe an action which is necessary, or a legal obligation, use *have to* or *need to*.
   You **have to** wear a seat belt when you are driving.
   We **need to** complete our tax form before 5th April.

2 To describe an action which isn't necessary, use *don't / doesn't have to* or *don't / doesn't need to*.
   We **don't have to** work at weekends in our company.
   The report **doesn't have to** be finished today.

3 For an action which is possible or permitted by law, use *can* or *allowed to*.
   You **can** leave early today because we're not very busy.
   Companies are **allowed to** advertise alcohol after 10 p.m.

4 If the action isn't permitted, use *can't* or *am not / isn't / aren't allowed to*.
   Sorry, but you **can't** smoke here.
   Cyclists **aren't allowed to** use motorways.

FORM

1 To ask a question with *have to* or *need to*, use *do* or *does*.
   Do I **have to** write this report now?
   Does the company **need to** have quality certification?

2 To ask a question with *allowed to*, use *am / is / are*.
   Are cigarette companies **allowed to** advertise?
   Am I **allowed to** park here?

3 Questions with *can* begin with the word *can*.
   Can foreigners vote in national elections?
   Can I use my phone for personal calls?

---

1 Match the job descriptions with the job titles.

doctor   sales rep   security guard
accountant   ski instructor   air hostess

1 I am allowed to travel for free when I go on holiday. _____

2 I don't have to travel much in my job, but I have to be good with numbers. _____

3 I can't take my holidays in the winter and I need to find other work in the summer. _____

4 I am not allowed to talk about what my patients have told me. _____

5 I have to attend meetings and I need to negotiate the best prices. _____

6 I don't need to work when the company is open, but I have to do a lot of night work. _____

2 Complete the missing words in this guide for new employees, using a suitable form of *have to*, *need to*, *can*, or *allowed to*.

> **Working at FTC: Frequently Asked Questions**
>
> 1 Q Where <u>can I / am I allowed to</u> park my car?
>   A In the employee car park behind the main building.
>
> 2 Q _____ I _____ to wear formal clothes to work?
>   A No, you don't. Jeans and a shirt are fine.
>
> 3 Q What hours do I have to work?
>   A Everyone _____ _____ be in the company between 10 a.m. and 4 p.m. But you _____ _____ to choose when you start and finish work, e.g. 8.00 to 4.00, 10.00 to 6.00.
>
> 4 Q _____ I _____ to take my paid holiday when I want?
>   A Yes, but you have to take at least three weeks in the summer.
>
> 5 Q Who do I see if I have a problem with my contract?
>   A You _____ _____ speak to the HR Manager.
>
> 6 Q Can I use the Internet for personal research?
>   A You _____ use it during your lunch break, but you _____ _____ to use it during office hours.
>
> 7 Q Am I allowed to use my office phone for private calls?
>   A You can make local calls to landlines and you _____ _____ to pay for these. You _____ use the office phone for long-distance calls or calls to mobiles.
>
> 8 Q _____ friends or family _____ to use the company canteen?
>   A No, they aren't. It's reserved for employees of the company.

61

BEC PRACTICE TEST

READING

PART 1

- Look at questions **1–5**.
- In each question, which phrase or sentence is correct?
- For each question, choose one letter (**A**, **B**, or **C**).

1

> It was agreed that Jonas will:
> - look at ways of cutting spending
> - talk to the bank about a loan
> - aim to balance the books in six months

Jonas will need to arrange a phone call / meeting to discuss

A the company's income and expenditure in the last six months.
B the possibility of borrowing some money.
C the amount of money the company is spending.

2

> **Sunhills community project**
> Completed: wiring and plumbing
> Ongoing: plastering and tiling
> Still to do: decorating and furnishing

The following project tasks are now finished

A painting the walls.
B putting tables and chairs in position.
C installing the toilets and sinks.

3

> **June**
> 5 June: complete decorating
> 6 June: safety checks
> 10 June: official opening

On the 9 June, what will have been completed?

A The safety checks.
B The decorating and the safety checks.
C The decorating, the safety checks, and the opening.

4

> Venue: €2,000
> Catering: €4,000
> Transport: €350
> Total: €6,350

The most expensive part of the project is

A the cars and vans.
B the food and drink.
C the rent for the building.

5

> Accomplished in bookkeeping.
> Knows how to operate a variety of computer software.
> Speaks English and Spanish.

Applicants must

A have customer service experience.
B be able to program computers.
C have bookkeeping experience.

PART 2

- Look at the advert below. It describes how this project management company can help you.
- For questions 1–5, decide which section (**A–I**) in the list is most suitable for each person.
- For each question, choose the correct letter (**A–I**).
- Do not use any letter more than once.

> Need help with project managing the opening of your new restaurant / bar? We can help in the following areas:
>
> A Obtaining finance
> B Calculating costs
> C Finding the best location
> D Organizing safety checks
> E Recruiting reliable electricians
> F Managing your accounts
> G Recruiting interior designers
> H Marketing and promotions
> I Organizing the official opening

1 Tobias Schmidt needs help in choosing the right building for his restaurant.
2 Maria Ronaldo needs someone to advise her on how to decorate and furnish her bar.
3 Vincent Lemaire wants some help with finding the best bank loan to fund his new restaurant.
4 Marco Morgese needs someone to fit the lights and install the ovens in his restaurant.
5 Faisal Alsubai would like to know where to advertise his restaurant.

BEC PRACTICE TEST

PART 3

- Look at the graphs below. They show the number of male and female customers in eight different fitness centres over a ten-year period.
- Which graph does each sentence (1–5) describe?
- For each sentence, choose one letter (A–H).
- Do not use any letter more than once.

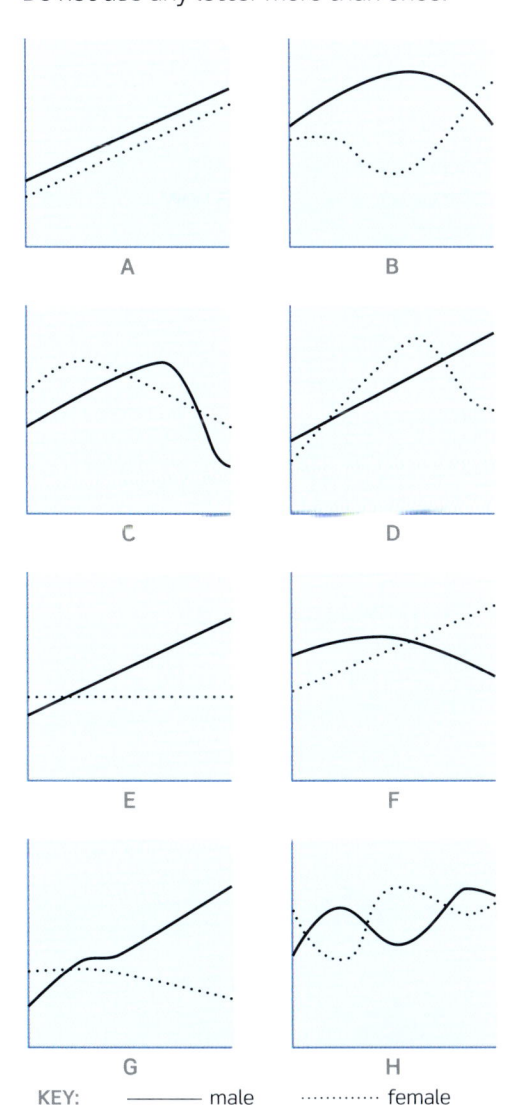

A B C D E F G H

KEY: ——— male ·········· female

1 The number of female customers remained steady, whilst the number of male customers rose steadily.
2 There has been a dramatic fall in both male and female customers.
3 There have been more male customers than female customers throughout the ten-year period.
4 The number of female customers decreased during the first part of the ten-year period and then increased in the second part of the ten-year period.
5 There has been a steady increase in the number of female customers, whilst the number of male customers has fallen.

PART 4

- Read the text below about volunteerism.
- Are sentences 1-7 'Right' or 'Wrong'? If there is not enough information to answer 'Right' or 'Wrong', choose 'Doesn't say'.
- For each sentence 1-7, choose one letter (A, B, or C).

A commitment to volunteerism

Volunteerism – what does it mean?

The clothing manufacturer, Timberland, is one of many large companies that are committed to volunteerism. The company encourages staff to spend up to 40 paid hours a year on community and social projects. The community benefits from the company's resources, staff gain new skills, and teamwork improves.

The French food manufacturer, Danone, allows its employees to spend time in developing countries, working on projects in areas like conservation, teaching, caring, or building. In doing so, they can share their own skills, and at the same time, they gain new ideas and insights, and learn from the experiences of others.

A team from the banking group, HBOS, volunteered to help build an extension to a school in La Esperanza in Honduras. Linda Marshall, the project leader, said, 'I learnt that when new teams are forming, it is essential that objectives are agreed and everyone buys in to them. This is a crucial factor to any project's success.'

What can volunteering do for you?

Software engineer, Samira Khan, is in charge of a volunteer project to redecorate a community centre for the elderly in Chicago. Managing a project is a new experience for her. She is learning how to organize a schedule so that they are able to complete the project before its deadline. She also has to deal with the budget, which is fairly limited, so she has to spend carefully. And every few days, she gets updates from her project team to check on progress and decide if they need more resources. She finds working on this project very rewarding and is pleased to be learning new skills.

1 Timberland employees do not receive a salary for the 40 hours they work on community and social projects.
A Right B Wrong C Doesn't say

2 Employees at Danone are allowed to spend 12 months working on a project in a developing country.
A Right B Wrong C Doesn't say

BEC PRELIMINARY

BEC PRACTICE TEST

3 Linda Marshall believes it is important that all team members accept the project aims.
 A Right B Wrong C Doesn't say

4 Samira Khan is receiving training on how to organize a project schedule.
 A Right B Wrong C Doesn't say

5 There is more than enough money available to spend on Samira's project.
 A Right B Wrong C Doesn't say

6 Team members regularly inform Samira about what is happening with the project.
 A Right B Wrong C Doesn't say

7 Samira is looking forward to starting work on a new project soon.
 A Right B Wrong C Doesn't say

PART 5

- Read the article below about Dell and answer the questions.
- For each question 1–6, choose one letter (A, B, or C).

Dell does it differently

Conventional manufacturers have to keep supplies of raw materials in order to produce their goods. Ordinary retailers too, have to keep the appropriate stock levels to satisfy their clients' needs. Enormous sums of money are tied up in this inventory. By contrast, Dell only builds once it has received an order and delivery takes, on average, seven to ten working days from the date the order is placed. By dealing directly with consumers through mail-shots, advertisements, and the Internet, it bypasses distributors and shopkeepers. And Dell's performance is truly breathtaking: its factories construct 80,000 machines per day and it can operate without warehouses. When an order is placed, the firm orders components from their suppliers. In addition, suppliers are expected to give credit even though Dell is paid in advance. This means that Dell has already been paid by its customers before it has to pay its own bills. Everything is so streamlined that it demands expert logistics and management of the supply chain.

1 According to the text, most retailers need to
 A order raw materials to keep their clients happy.
 B have a number of unsold products available for sale.
 C store appropriate supplies from manufacturers.

2 Dell is an unusual retailer because
 A it waits for an order before producing a product.
 B orders take seven to ten working days to arrive at the company.
 C products are delivered on the same day they are ordered.

3 Dell contacts potential customers
 A through distributors and shopkeepers.
 B through distributors, shopkeepers, mailshots, adverts, and the Internet.
 C through mailshots, adverts, and the Internet.

4 Dell is very successful and
 A now employs 80,000 factory workers.
 B operates from several warehouses.
 C doesn't need storage areas for its stock.

5 When a customer order is received,
 A suppliers order components from Dell.
 B clients order through Dell's suppliers.
 C Dell orders components from the suppliers.

6 The first exchange of money is when
 A Dell pays the suppliers.
 B the customer pays Dell.
 C the customer pays the suppliers.

BEC PRACTICE TEST

PART 6

- Read the text below about the Breakthrough Café.
- Choose the correct word to fill each gap, from **A**, **B**, or **C**.
- For each question **1–12**, choose one letter (**A**, **B**, or **C**).

The Breakthrough Café is the brainchild ¹_____ Mitchell Ditkoff and John Havens. The aim is that customers will have ²_____ least one 'a-ha' moment during an evening ³_____ is a combination of 'party, restaurant, and brainstorming session'.

Over a three-course meal, customers begin by ⁴_____ each other and reading their name badges. The name badge ⁵_____ contains the words 'How can I ... ?'. Each customer completes this ⁶_____ a question about an idea or obstacle in their life. For example, 'How can I start my own catering business?', 'How can I find someone ⁷_____ in my prototype?', 'How can I get ⁸_____ new job?'. As well ⁹_____ discussing and giving advice to each other, there are 'Innowaiters' ¹⁰_____ serve food and drink, but also act as facilitators to encourage innovative ideas.

Ditkoff explains how he first came ¹¹_____ with the concept. 'I've asked thousands of people: "Where do you get your best ideas? What is the catalyst?" Less than one per cent of people say they get their ideas at work. They get their ideas when they are happy, away from the office, late at night, and in the company ¹²_____ friends.'

1 A from   B of   C on
2 A the   B a   C at
3 A what   B where   C that
4 A meeting   B meet   C to meet
5 A and   B also   C with
6 A with   B from   C about
7 A investing B invests   C to invest
8 A the   B a   C some
9 A like   B as   C than
10 A who   B which   C what
11 A over   B out   C up
12 A of   B from   C with

PART 7

- Read the memo and the letter below.
- Complete the order form.
- Write a word or phrase for each section **1–5**.

MEMO

From: John Ritchie
To: Caron Edwards

Can you complete the order form for this email from Abracomp?

Thanks

Dear Sir / Madam

I would like to place an order for 2,000 motherboards. This is a repeat order. We need these urgently so please send them asap. Please charge it to our account as usual.

Kind regards

Gisele Kern

Order form

1 Company name: _____
2 Name of contact at company: _____
3 New customer?: _____
4 Product: _____
5 Quantity: _____

BEC PRACTICE TEST

WRITING

PART 1

- You work in the Marketing Department of your company. You are going to interview an applicant for a vacancy in the department.
- Write an **email** to your administrator, including the following information:
  - what the applicant's name is
  - which vacancy she has applied for
  - when she should come for an interview.
- Write **30-40** words.

PART 2

- Read this email from a health spa you have contacted.

To: xxx
From: Melanie Gilbert
Subject: Booking confirmation GWS0012Y

Dear Customer

I am writing to confirm your two days at Limewood Spa. The Spa expects you on the evening of Thursday 12th. Your personal trainer is meeting you at 9.00 a.m. on the Friday morning. He will assess your needs and provide you with a plan to ensure that you make the most of your stay with us. If you are interested in booking any of our other facilities, please check our website and online booking system.

We look forward to seeing you and I hope you have a pleasant stay.

Best wishes

Melanie Gilbert
Limewood Spa

- Write an **email** to Melanie Gilbert:
  - thanking her for the confirmation
  - checking that the booking is for a double room (not a single)
  - asking if breakfast is included in the price
  - asking about the facilities in the room.
- Write **60-80** words.

BEC PRACTICE TEST

LISTENING

PART 1

- For questions **1–8**, you will hear two phone conversations (there are four questions for each conversation).
- For each question, choose one letter (**A**, **B**, or **C**).
- Listen to the recordings twice.

A ▶ BEC 1

1 Why is Ms Kern calling Composource?
   A To place an order.
   B To cancel an order.
   C To enquire about an order.

2 What information does the caller have to give?
   A Her email address.
   B Her account number.
   C The order number.

3 When was the order sent from the warehouse?
   A The 11th February.
   B The 12th February.
   C The 13th February.

4 What does Linda say she'll do?
   A Fix the problem herself.
   B Call the warehouse.
   C Go to the warehouse.

A ▶ BEC 2

5 What happened two weeks ago?
   A The warehouse dispatched the order.
   B The warehouse lost the order.
   C The customer changed the order.

6 What information had the customer given on the order?
   A To send the items by courier.
   B To send the items as quickly as possible.
   C No specific information.

7 What does the caller request?
   A To cancel the order.
   B A discount of £400.
   C A new order of 400 units.

8 When will Linda call the customer back?
   A In the next 60 minutes.
   B Immediately.
   C After 60 minutes.

PART 2

- Look at the notes below.
- Some information is missing.
- You will hear a voicemail message.
- For each question **1–6**, fill in the missing information in the numbered space using a **word**, **numbers**, or **letters**.
- Listen to the recording twice.

A ▶ BEC 3

CALLER: Linda, Composource
DATE: 1 _____
TIME OF CALL: 2 _____
MESSAGE: 400 motherboards sent by 3 _____ today.
EXPECTED DELIVERY DATE: 4 _____
REFERENCE NUMBER: 5 _____

Supplier is very 6 _____ for original problems.

PART 3

- Look at the notes about a presentation.
- Some information is missing.
- You will hear the presenter telling managers about something new for their company.
- For each question **1–7**, fill in the missing information in the space using one or two words.
- Listen to the recording twice.

A ▶ BEC 4

- Reason for presentation = new 1 _____
- How long until it can be used in all hotels: a 2 _____
- Staff will need 3 _____ before they can use it.
- The bottom section on the screen is 4 _____ from the old database.
- It gives customers what they want and makes it 5 _____ to handle a booking for a return customer.
- Drop-down menus mean you can 6 _____ the information when you take the booking.
- Another advantage: customers can now book 7 _____

BEC PRELIMINARY

BEC PRACTICE TEST

PART 4

- You will hear a meeting and then an interview.
- For each question **1–8**, choose one letter (**A**, **B**, or **C**) for the correct answer.
- Listen to the recordings twice.

A ▶ BEC 5

1 What does Dieter think about the 'two-camps' mentality?
  A It tends to happen with every merger.
  B It can be completely avoided.
  C It will ruin Nikos's plans.

2 What is Nikos planning to do to help the merger be successful?
  A Organize a team-building session with two camps competing against each other.
  B Ask staff to start working together immediately.
  C Organize informal sessions where staff can get to know each other.

3 What does Carmen say about the big event for everybody?
  A She needs some suggestions about what should happen.
  B She already knows what she wants to happen.
  C She wants the event to be very formal.

4 What is Carmen's conclusion about the merger?
  A There will be lots of difficulties that will continue for a long time.
  B There will be disagreements and arguments every day between the two sides.
  C Initially there will be some difficulties, but after a while everything will be fine.

A ▶ BEC 6

5 Steve's company is
  A exactly like Dell.
  B a lot smaller than Dell.
  C a bit smaller than Dell.

6 The main advantage for Steve's company is
  A being able to offer the customer a face-to-face service.
  B keeping a lot of components in stock.
  C having barcodes on everything and using a database.

7 What does the database do if there is only one of a particular component left in stock?
  A It immediately creates an order for that component.
  B It informs Steve or his staff about the situation.
  C It finds out whether that component is obsolete.

8 Steve thinks the tracking facility is
  A essential to his business.
  B useful for very important items.
  C not worth bothering with.

BEC PRACTICE TEST

SPEAKING

PART 1
Practise answering these questions:
- What is your name?
- Do you work or study?
- Describe your current job or your dream job.
- Describe your ideal holiday.

PART 2
- Choose **one** of two topics and prepare a short talk (about 5 minutes) on it.

CANDIDATE A

> A **What is important in a job?**
> - Money
> - Job satisfaction
> - Variety

> B **What security measures are important for a business?**
> - Security staff
> - Staff ID cards
> - CCTV

CANDIDATE B

> A **What is important for an office building?**
> - Modern furniture
> - Staff restaurant
> - Central location

> B **What should you remember when preparing for a business trip?**
> - Flight times
> - Hotel details
> - What to take

PART 3
- Practise discussing this task, and the questions that come after it, with a partner:

> During a team-building training session, you are asked to discuss attitudes towards success in life. Decide which three of the following five topics are most connected to success?
> - Money and wealth
> - Qualifications
> - Good personal relationships
> - Good job / career
> - Good health

Follow-up discussion questions:
- Are successful people always happy? Why? / Why not?
- Who are the most successful people you know?
- Why are they so successful?
- Do you think qualifications automatically lead to a more successful life?

AUDIO AND VIDEO SCRIPTS

MODULE 1

1.1
Receptionist Life Health Clubs. How can I help?
George Hi. This is George Lawrence. I'm calling from Washington. Could I speak to the Marketing Director, please?
Receptionist I'm afraid he's in a meeting all day. Can I take a message, Mr Lawrence?
George How about the Sales Director?
Receptionist Hold the line, please ... I'm sorry Mr Lawrence, but his line is busy. Can I help?
George Well, I'm trying to arrange a visit to your company for an article I'm writing on health clubs around the world.
Receptionist In that case I'll put you through to our Public Relations Department. One second, please.
Marie-Claire Public Relations. Marie-Claire speaking. How can I help?

1.2
1
Cathy Hello. Could I speak to Lars Johannsen, please?
Receptionist I'm afraid he's not at his desk right now. Can I take a message?
Cathy Yes, could you ask him to call me back, please? It's Cathy Lamble from Toronto. I'd like to arrange a meeting for next month.
Receptionist Could you give me your number, please?
Cathy Yes, it's 01 5487 29445.

2
Jean-Pierre Good morning. I'd like to speak to Gavan Bix, please.
Receptionist Who's calling, please?
Jean-Pierre It's Jean-Pierre Gauvain from Paris.
Receptionist I'm afraid he's talking on another line.
Jean-Pierre Can you give him a message for me, then?
Receptionist Yes, certainly.
Jean-Pierre Could you tell him I called and ask him if he agrees with a three per cent price rise on all our products from January?
Receptionist Of course.

3
Caller Hi, is Rachel there?
Receptionist No, sorry, she must be at lunch. Shall I leave her a message?
Caller No, I'll call back in about three quarters of an hour.
Receptionist OK.

4
Jean Good afternoon. I'd like to speak to the manager, please.
Receptionist I'm afraid he's in a meeting. Who shall I say called?
Jean It's Jean Tan. You've sent us a bill for $369.50 and it can't be right. Please tell him to call me back urgently.

1.3
Hi, this is María José Fernández. It's four o'clock on Monday the 12th. I was just calling about your order. I have a few questions to ask you. Could you please call me back? You can reach me on 07892 159753. Thanks.

1.4
Kiko Good morning. On Spot Media.
Robert Oh, hello Kiko. It's ... from *Interview* magazine.
Kiko I'm sorry, who's calling? Can you repeat your name, please?
Robert Yes, it's Robert Phillips from *Interview* magazine.
Kiko I'm very sorry, I still didn't catch your name. Could you say it again, please?
Robert Kiko, it's Robert – from *Interview*.
Kiko Oh yes, Robert. Of course. How are you?
Robert A bit busy, but apart from that ...
Kiko Excuse me a moment, Robert, I've got another call.
...
Kiko Robert. Sorry about that. What can I do for you?
Robert Don't worry, Kiko. Can I have extension
...
Kiko Robert? I'm afraid I can't hear you. Robert?
...
Kiko On Spot Media.
Robert It's me, Robert, again.
Kiko Oh, I'm sorry about that, Robert. I think we got cut off. Who did you want to speak to?
Robert Can you put me through to Yuichiro on extension 3390, please?
Kiko Can I have the number again, please?
Robert Yes, it's 3390.
Kiko Thanks. I'll put you straight through.

1.5
1
Caller I'd like to speak to Matti, please.
Receptionist I'm sorry, there isn't a Matti in this office.

2
Caller Ich möchte bitte mit Claudia sprechen.
Receptionist I'm afraid I don't understand. Do you speak English?

3
Caller Oh hello. It's Mehmet here.
Receptionist I'm sorry, who's calling? Can you repeat your name, please?

4
Caller It's about the project.
Receptionist Excuse me a moment, Mehmet, I've got another call.

5
Caller Hello, it's Mehmet again. We were speaking a minute ago.
Receptionist Oh, I'm sorry about that, Mehmet. I think we got cut off.

6
Caller I wanted to talk to Stuart about the JW111.
Receptionist I'm sorry. I'm not sure I understand.

1.6
Fenola Hello. Is that Michael Wan?
Michael Speaking.
Fenola Hello, Michael. It's Fenola Young here from GW Architects.
Michael Hello, Fenola. How can I help you?
Fenola I'd like to meet you some time next week to discuss our ideas for the new software application.
Michael Yes, of course. When are you available?
Fenola Does Tuesday morning suit you?
Michael I'm afraid I'm not available on Tuesday. Shall we say Wednesday at 11.00 instead?
Fenola Yes, that suits me. Thank you so much.
Michael Thank you. So that's Wednesday at 11.00, then.
Fenola Yes. Goodbye.

1.7
Fenola Hi. Sven?
Sven Hi, Fenola. How's it going?
Fenola Not too bad. Listen. Can we meet for lunch next week?
Sven Great idea. When are you free?
Fenola Is Tuesday OK for you?
Sven Sorry, I can't make it on Tuesday. How about Thursday at 12.30 instead?
Fenola Sounds good. Same place as usual?
Sven Yes. Same place at 12.30. See you then.
Fenola See you on Thursday. Bye.

1.8
Sergio Yes, of course. Actually, we're coming to Switzerland next month.
Elena Really?
Sergio Yes, we already have another client in Zurich. Is that near you?
Elena Not too far. I'm in Bern. It's only a couple of hours away.

AUDIO AND VIDEO SCRIPTS

Sergio Fine. Can we arrange a meeting then?
Elena Sure.
Sergio Let's see. Well, my trip begins on the 30th of January. That's a Monday. How about Tuesday the 31st?
Elena I'd prefer the Wednesday.
Sergio The 1st of February? Yes, that suits me.

1.9
Elena Hello. Elena Schenker speaking.
Sergio Hello, Elena. This is Sergio Lanese from Technogym.
Elena Hello. Nice to hear from you again.
Sergio How are things?
Elena Fine, thanks.
Sergio Sorry for calling so late in the day.
Elena That's OK. I've only just got back to the office.
Sergio Is this a busy time for you?
Elena Yes, the ski season is our busiest time of year.
Sergio Of course. Is there plenty of snow? What's the weather like?
Elena There's a lot of snow, which is good. It's snowing right now, actually.
Sergio Good. I'm actually calling about my visit. I'm afraid I've just realized I can't make the Wednesday. Can we move the meeting back to Thursday?
Elena OK ... yes, the afternoon is free.
Sergio Great – there's a train that arrives at 12.30. So after lunch? At 2.00?
Elena OK. Two o'clock, then.
Sergio Thank you. Sorry about that, I have an extra meeting on the Wednesday.
Elena No problem. See you then.
Sergio OK, thanks. Bye.
Elena Bye.

1.10
Elaine So Harriet ... Do you think you'll be able to finish the flyer by the end of the month?
Harriet Yes. I think I can manage to do it by then.
Elaine Fine. I'll send you an email with the details, then.
Harriet Great. That'll be good. Do I have to sign a contract for the job?
Elaine Yes, you can come and sign the contract whenever you have time. Thanks for everything, Harriet.
Harriet Right. No problem.
Elaine Don't forget to call me if you've got any questions about my email.
Harriet OK. I could call you back when I've read it, if you want.
Elaine Right. We'll speak later, then.
Harriet OK. I'll call you some time after 5.00.

Elaine Fine. I should be here.
Harriet Talk then.
Elaine Great. Bye, then.
Harriet Bye.

MODULE 2

2.1
Gianluca Excuse me. Is this seat free?
Jana Yes, it is. Go ahead.
Gianluca Thanks very much. Can I introduce myself? I'm Gianluca Donatelli.
Jana Nice to meet you. I am Jana Frkova.
Gianluca Nice to meet you too, Jana. Where are you from?
Jana I am from the Czech Republic. But I work all over Europe.
Gianluca And who do you work for?
Jana I don't work for a company. I am self-employed.
Gianluca Oh really? And what do you do?
Jana I am a journalist. I write articles for consumer magazines.
Gianluca So why are you at this conference?
Jana I am here to research an article on Internet service providers.
Gianluca That's interesting. A friend of mine works for an Italian service provider. Can I introduce you to him?
Jana Yes, of course. That would be nice.
Gianluca Roberto. Can you come here for a minute? This is ... Sorry, what's your name again?
Jana Jana. Jana Frkova.
Gianluca Roberto. This is Jana. She's writing an article on Internet service providers.

2.2
1
Gianluca What do you do?
Jana I am a journalist. I write articles for consumer magazines. What about you? What do you do?
Gianluca I'm a sales manager.

2
Gianluca Why are you at this conference?
Jana I'm here to research an article on Internet service providers. What about you? What are you here for?
Gianluca We want to find new customers in the European market.

2.3
Dan Excuse me. Are you Jozef Dropinski?
Jozef Yes, I am. And you must be Dan Ford.
Dan That's right. Pleased to meet you, Jozef.
Jozef Nice to meet you, Dan.
Dan OK, then. Let's go and get a taxi.

Jozef Right. I'll follow you.
Dan OK, the taxis are outside, about two minutes' walk from here. So, did you have a good flight, Jozef?
Jozef Hmm, it was delayed for half an hour, but apart from that, everything was fine.
Dan Well, I suppose half an hour isn't so bad. Do you often travel abroad on business?
Jozef Probably about once a month, really. Last month I was in Granada.
Dan Really! Granada's beautiful, isn't it?
Jozef Yes, it is. Have you been there, then?
Dan Yes, I went there with my wife for a weekend a couple of years ago. Did you see the Alhambra?
Jozef Yes, fortunately we had time to do a bit of sightseeing, so I went to have a look.
Dan What did you think of it?
Jozef I thought it was beautiful. And really peaceful too. In fact, I loved it.
Dan The architecture is amazing, isn't it? Are you interested in architecture, Jozef?
Jozef To be honest, I don't really know much about it, but I do enjoy visiting new places when I can. What about you?
Dan Yes, me too, but I've only got time to travel during the holidays. When do you usually take your holiday?
Jozef I usually have a fortnight in the summer and a week in early spring. How about you?
Dan I always go skiing for a week in February.
Jozef Do you? Where do you usually go?
Dan To Andorra. There are some excellent ski slopes there. Can you ski?
Jozef Yes. I really enjoy it. Last year we went to Slovenia in March. It was brilliant, and there was plenty of snow.
Dan Well, here are the taxis. Let's get in the queue.

VIDEO 1
It's Maria's first day at QPG. She is waiting for her manager, Paul.

Monica Hi, Maria!
Maria Hello again, Monica.
Monica Is everything OK? Can I help you with something?
Maria Oh, no thanks. It's fine. I'm waiting for Paul. My induction finished early.
Monica Oh right. Well it's my break now. Can I join you?
Maria Yes, of course. Take a seat.
Monica Actually, I want to get a coffee. Can I get you something?
Maria Um ... OK, yeah. I'll have a latte, please.
Monica Why don't you come with me? I'll show you where to get it.
...

AUDIO AND VIDEO SCRIPTS

MODULE 2

Maria So how long have you worked here?
Monica Nearly a year now. It's a good company – nice people generally.
Maria Do you know most of the people here, then?
Monica Well, I am the receptionist, so I see them coming and going every day. I don't know all of them, but I know most of their faces.
Maria How many people work here?
Monica Ooh, I'm not sure ... lots. I don't know. The HR Department will know. Oh, you are in the HR Department! I should ask you that question!
Maria Well, the Training Department really, and it is only my first day.
Monica I know, I'm joking. So what do you think of it, anyway?
Maria Well it seems very nice. Good coffee!
Monica Yes, we're lucky. So what did you do before?
Maria I worked in the HR Department of an accountancy company.
Monica Which one?
Maria Oh, a small one. It's called Reynolds and Waters.
Monica No! I worked for them too. About three years ago. Wow, what a coincidence!
Maria Ha! Poor you!
Monica I know! It wasn't a great organization. I understand why you came here now!
Paul Must be a good joke!
Monica Oh. Hi, Paul! Right, I'll leave you to it. Nice talking to you again.
Maria Yes, you too! Bye.
Paul Sorry I'm late. How was your induction?
Maria Oh fine, thanks.
Paul Good. Well, how about we hang up your coat and I'll show you around?
Maria Great.

2.4

1
A So, here we are. This is your hotel.
B Thanks very much for picking me up at the airport.
A My pleasure. Just before you go, some of us are meeting for dinner tonight. Would you like to join us?
B Thanks for the invitation, but I'm exhausted. I think I'll just get something in the hotel and then have an early night. I'll see you tomorrow. Good night.

2
A Please take a seat.
B Thanks.
A Shall I get you a glass of water?
B Yes, please. That would be nice.

3
A Hello. Samantha, isn't it?
B Yes, that's right.
A Hi. I'm Filip. Would you like a coffee?
B No, thanks. I'd rather have tea.

4
A Did you know the Chinese State Circus is in town?
B No, I didn't. Oh, I love them. I've seen them three times.
A Well, would you like me to book a ticket for you?
B Yes, please. That's very kind of you.

2.5

Conversation 1
A Would you like a drink?
B No thanks, I'm fine.

Conversation 2
A Do you fancy a drink?
B That would be great, thanks.

Conversation 3
A Would you like a drink?
B Yes, please. A coffee would be nice.

Conversation 4
A Can I get you a drink?
B A drink sounds good.

Conversation 5
A Do you fancy a drink?
B I'd love one.

Conversation 6
A Do you want a drink?
B I'm afraid I don't have time.

2.6

Marvin Hello, I'm Marvin Bernstein. I have an appointment with Jacinta Ross.
Jacinta Hi, I'm Jacinta. Welcome to our new facility.
Marvin Thank you. It's nice to be here.
Jacinta It's nice to finally meet you in person.
Marvin Likewise.
Jacinta So, how was your journey?
Marvin It was fine. There was quite a lot of traffic.
Jacinta Ah. And did you have any trouble finding us?
Marvin No, not at all, your directions were excellent.
Jacinta I'm glad to hear it. Here, let me take your coat.
Marvin Uh, that's OK. I'll hang on to it if you don't mind.
Jacinta Of course not. Uh, can I get you a coffee, or would you like to freshen up a bit?
Marvin A coffee sounds nice.
Jacinta OK. Come this way and I'll run through today's programme. Here you are. Have a seat.
Marvin Thanks.
Jacinta So, first of all, I thought you could join a tour of the facility this morning. Aruna Singh is showing some people around. Then, we'll catch up again at lunchtime, and after that, I'll introduce you to the team.
Marvin And will I be seeing Dilip Patel today?
Jacinta He's introducing the tour this morning, but you'll get a chance to meet up with him over lunch.
Marvin Great.
Jacinta Now, remember, you'll need this ID card to get around the site. Make sure you keep it on you at all times.
Marvin No problem. And what about my car? Am I allowed to leave it in the staff car park?
Jacinta Yes. Don't worry about that. I'll clear it with Facilities. What's your registration number?
Marvin It's ...

2.7

Dilip Good morning everyone. My name is Dilip Patel, and I'm the head of public relations. On behalf of JJP Electronics, it gives me great pleasure to welcome you to our facility. We're going to begin with a guided tour. Afterwards, you will have the opportunity to meet our engineers over lunch. I'd now like to introduce you to Aruna Singh who is going to show you around the plant. Before I hand you over to Aruna, can I remind you that this is a working factory. So for your own safety, please be sure to stay with her at all times. May I wish you all an enjoyable and instructive visit.
Aruna Thank you, Dilip. Good morning, everyone. If you'd like to follow me, we'll begin the tour.

2.8

1 In the office
John Hi Fran. Hey, do you want some help?
Fran No, it's fine thanks, John. It's just ... well ... where are the new books on Austria?
John They're in the other office. I'll just get them.
Fran OK. Thanks. I want to pack up all the boxes first, and then, I'll do the brochures, and after that I'll put the T-shirts and pens out.

2 At the car
Fran Oh dear. We've got so many things. Do you think there's room for everything?
John Yes, of course! Wait. Let me help. First of all, I'll put the back seat down. Then we can put these boxes in. OK?

AUDIO AND VIDEO SCRIPTS

Fran And the laptop?
John We can put it on top, here. Right? Now there's lots of space. See?
Fran And the posters?
John Don't worry. There's plenty of room. Leave it to me. I'll bring them down from the office afterwards.

3 Setting up the stand
John Oh hello, Fran. You're here early. Are you doing OK?
Fran Of course I am. There's just a lot to do, isn't there?
John Yes. Do you want a hand?
Fran No, no. It's fine.
John Well, why don't I empty the boxes?
Fran No, really. I can do it myself. I'll do the boxes first, and then do the table.
John Come on. How can I help?
Fran It's all fine, I think.
John How about a coffee. Shall I get one for you?
Fran No. I haven't got time.
John Right. OK. Just one for me, then. Oh, and, Fran, very nice T-shirt, but it's back to front!
Fran Oh no! Thanks.

4 The end of the trade fair
John Well. Everyone's gone home, and all the freebies have gone!
Fran Yep. Oh, I'm so tired! Look! It's quite late already.
John Listen, can I get you a drink? There's a pub over the road.
Fran No, no. Not yet. I want to clear up these things. First I'll put all the books back in the boxes, and after that I'll …
John Fran! Not now. We can do it together later.
Fran Oh. All right then. Actually, a large beer would be great!

2.9
Simon OK, well, I was in London a few years ago on a business trip, and I was flying back home to the States from Heathrow, and I could see that the plane was going to be really full. I mean, people were lining up for miles.
Mark Overbooking, right?
Simon Exactly, and I could see these two ground staff.
Gina Oh yes.
Simon They were coming down the line, asking everybody at check-in a question. Can you guess what it was?
Gina No.
Mark Me neither.
Simon They were asking everybody, very politely 'Because this flight to New York is overbooked, would you mind flying tomorrow instead of today?'
Mark And what did you say?
Simon Well, I could see that there were families on vacation, there were sports teams and so on, and they probably had a tighter schedule than me. And I was going home, so a day earlier, a day later, what the heck.
Gina And that's what you told them?
Simon No, I said: 'It would be very inconvenient for me not to take this flight today, but if you don't find anyone, come back and talk to me again …'

2.10
Simon And guess what? They couldn't find anyone else: the families couldn't wait a day, neither could the sports teams.
Gina But you were more flexible?
Simon I knew if they came back, the situation would be worse. So I told them: 'As I said before, it's not convenient for me to miss this flight, but you can put me on tomorrow's flight if you upgrade my seat to first class.'
Gina Hey, that was good! You …
Simon Hang on, I'm not finished yet. 'You upgrade my seat to first class, give me a four-star hotel in London tonight, and £150 in cash'.
Mark Wow! First class, a four-star hotel, and £150!
Gina And did they?
Simon What do you think? They agreed immediately.
Mark I think you're smarter than I am, Simon.
Simon Just more experienced at travelling, Mark.
Gina And then?
Simon Well, I phoned home and told my wife I'd be getting home one day later than planned.
Gina Did she mind?
Simon Mind? Hey, she met me at the airport with her lawyer!

2.11
1
Good morning and welcome to the annual conference of Wired 2 Play Entertainment Ltd. My name is Thorsten Richter and I'm head of the European division. I've been with the company for fifteen years, and last year I was promoted to this position. In my previous role I ran the Creative Department in Bonn where we developed the best-selling games 'Riders in the Storm' and 'Kingdom Come'.
Over the last year I've met with all the country managers to discuss our falling sales figures. At the moment we're working together with a consultant, Amy Chang, to analyse our main problems. In the future we may have to target a different market to increase sales. I'd be grateful for any ideas you might have here. So, that's enough about me. Let me tell you about those sales figures I mentioned …

2
Right then, before I start, I'll tell you a bit about myself. My name's Amy Chang and I'm a freelance consultant. I studied economics and business at Beijing University from 2002 to 2005 and after doing my MBA, I joined PricewaterhouseCoopers. I left Price when I had the opportunity to go freelance.
Recently I have worked on several successful cases with clients of yours, which is how I came into contact with your company. Up to now I've managed to find solutions for all the companies I've worked with.
In my current role as consultant to your company, I'm looking to improve your sales figures and reduce your costs. Over the next year I'll spend two weeks in each department before I sit down and write my recommendations report. I'm looking forward to working with all of you.

MODULE 3
VIDEO 2

Glasbau Hahn is a glass-making factory in Frankfurt in Germany. Till Hahn is its Director.

Our company has been based from the very start always in Frankfurt am Main. Originally we had been more in the centre of the city but during World War II Frankfurt was heavily bombed and then we moved out a bit towards the East, and this is where we are and where we feel very happy.
We can trace our company back to 1836, that's when my great grandfather came to Frankfurt as a glazier and he married a widow who had been in the glass business already before, and ever since it's in the hands of the Hahns.
Our company can be divided in three sections – the original one was strictly the glass business, windows, door fronts, glass doors and so on, er … the second one is louvered windows – the special window for ventilation. Perhaps the most glamorous part of our business is display cases and museum equipment.

Who are your clients?
Well when I talk about display cases, our clients certainly, are museums … museums, all around the world, after England we were brave enough to expand into the United States, that was my special effort for the company, which has

MODULE 3

AUDIO AND VIDEO SCRIPTS

turned out very well and now we are doing business er ... with most places on earth. We have, I think, six offices for representing us, spread around.

How many employees do you have?
In Frankfurt we have about 120 employees. There are about another 35 in Stockstadt, who are doing the louvered window business, and then we have about another 15 people in our various offices in Japan, in Tokyo, er ... in China, in the United States and in England.

Who are your competitors?
There had been some glorious times in the past when we didn't have any competition, that was in 1935 when my father invented the first all-glass construction, meaning the bonding of glass to glass without intermediate framing. Then, it was back in 1970 when competitors became more apparent and, er ... they are not so much in Germany but rather one of the competitors is based in Italy, one is in England, and we always meet when there is an international bidding to do, and usually we are the most expensive one but, fortunately, our clients nevertheless rank quality highest and the price tag is not the only decision factor, otherwise it would be very to our disadvantage. Our markets where we are very successful outside of England and America is lately ... especially, is Japan, very important, China and even Egypt.

3.1
James Which company do you work for?
Fiona It's called Besam. B-E-S-A-M. You probably don't know it.
James No, I don't. What does the company do?
Fiona We specialize in automatic door mechanisms. But we're a subsidiary of Assa Abloy. Perhaps you know that name?
James No, sorry. I don't.
Fiona It's a Swedish group. It makes locks and security systems. I'm sure you know some of our products. Yale locks ... or Chubb ... or Vachette, for example?
James No, I'm afraid I don't. Is it a very big group, then?
Fiona Yes, it is. There are about 30,000 employees.
James That is big.
Fiona And annual sales of about three billion euros.
James So are you mainly in the European market?
Fiona No, we operate in 40 different countries worldwide. There are 150 different companies in the Assa Abloy group.

James Who are your main competitors, then?
Fiona The Eastern Company? Ingersoll Rand? Master Lock?
James Well, I think you can see now that I know nothing about the security business.
Fiona So who do you work for?
James Microsoft.
Fiona And what does your company do?
James We make ... Ah, that's a joke, right?

3.2
1
In our department we do reports at the end of each month which show all the money going into and out of the company. It takes a really long time. I have a meeting today with Anna Neves, who's responsible for our software. She's coming to show me a new program she wants to buy. She says it will help us a lot with all our financial reporting.

2
Our company is divided into three business units: Home, Industrial, and Public Services. I work in the Industrial Business Unit. I organize all the transport from suppliers to our factories, and from our factories to customers. Today I have a visit from Ralf Ehrling. He's the person in charge of buying for the whole group. He wants to use just three or four big international transporters for all three of our business units. He thinks it will cost less to have a small number of suppliers.

3
I have contact with a lot of training organizations. We have a lot of people learning English here. We're also organizing a lot of IT courses this year, because we're changing our marketing software at the moment. I report to the HR Director. She's coming here for a meeting today. We're employing a lot of new people this year, and she thinks they have special training needs. We're talking about what courses we can offer them.

3.3
Interviewer Where do you work?
Sang Chun In the Technical Support Department.
Interviewer So what do you do exactly?
Sang Chun Basically, my job consists of answering calls from customers who are having problems with their software. But it also involves working with sales reps from time to time. We visit new customers together.
Interviewer Do you develop software too?
Sang Chun We aren't involved in developing new programs. But when programmers are preparing new versions of old products,

we take part in the discussions. We speak to customers every day, so we know the technical issues very well.
Interviewer So what sort of problems do you have to solve?
Sang Chun Oh, the usual. We deal with installation issues, password problems, bugs, things like that.

3.4
1 The problem with all these sites is that you have to book everything separately and it takes such a long time. It's also difficult to get exactly what you want because you can't see all the options. I can never seem to get a cheap deal.

2 I don't like using the cash machines outside because people walk past all the time. But if I go to a cashier, it takes so long to get information about my account because of the queues. And they're only open when I'm working, so I have to go during my lunchtime.

3 We really need to access all the latest news that is relevant to our business. The problem is, it takes so long to find what we want on all the different websites. And some of their search options are ... are really difficult to use.

3.5
1 They provide an excellent service. We can rely on them to deliver orders on time and that allows us to maintain excellent relationships with all our customers.

2 Being up to date with what's happening in the world is really important to me. And this also lets me know what's happening in the money markets, wherever I am. It also makes it easier to make quick decisions about what to buy and sell.

3 It's so much faster than going there and I don't have to worry if it is open or if there are a lot of other people. I just log on any time, and all I do is choose the products I want and give my credit card number. It really helps me to manage my time better.

4 I was so happy when it opened. It lets me work full-time and still have time with my child in the middle of the day.

3.6
Extract 1
A OK, everyone. What I want to do today, is to explain the new security procedures. I'll talk about the background to the situation, then I'll run through the principal changes. As you know, we've recently been having

AUDIO AND VIDEO SCRIPTS

a few problems with people just walking in off the street. Up to now, no one has stolen anything, but we obviously need to safeguard against that happening. Because of this, we've decided to upgrade the system. So, first I'd like to update you on the plans for changes to security procedures around the building …

Extract 2

A … So, as a result, we've been installing these electronic boxes on all the entrances around the building over the last few weeks. These are for a new swipe card system that will come into operation at the end of the month.

B Sorry, but what's the reason for changing the current system? How long has Security been having a problem with the system of badges?

A For quite a while, I'm afraid. We've had three incidents reported since the beginning of the month. It's because Security can't always check everyone's badge when they come in. By swiping these cards through these electronic readers on every door, we can check a person's identity anywhere in the building.

C Sorry, but I don't quite understand how they work. Can you tell us more about them?

A Mm. When you come to a door, you just swipe the card through this box at the side, and it opens.

B Do you mean that we have to swipe every time we want to go through a door?

A I'm afraid so, but the current situation, as it stands, simply doesn't prevent people from entering your office. By checking for identity at all the main doors, we hope to solve the problem, or at least make it safer.

VIDEO 3

The Human Resources departmental managers at Quartz Power Group have come to the end of their weekly team meeting. Before they finish, Paul, the HR Manager, gives a short presentation to the team.

Paul OK. Well before we finish, I had something I just wanted to talk about for a few moments. As you know, we are relocating and everyone is already asking how we are all going to work from a new building which doesn't have enough office space for everyone. And as the MD announced at his staff presentation, we are going to be implementing flexible working hours wherever possible, and also working from home if it suits certain members of staff to do so. This is a huge change to our company culture and of course to our administrative systems in terms of time-keeping and record keeping. So the MD would like someone to look into the whole process and make recommendations on how it can all be implemented. And guess who's got that job? Actually it isn't as bad as it sounds, but I'd like to ask you as a group to help me out on this. So basically, over the next few weeks, I'm going to be using part of these regular meetings to help with the planning. What we have is a three-part process. And part one of that process is 'Who?' Who can actually work flexible hours? Because it won't suit everyone and it won't be appropriate for certain jobs and roles.

And the next question is 'What?' What are we going to have to change? What will people have to do?

And finally … 'How?' How are we going to implement all these changes? People are going to have to change the way they think about this. Not just the staff, but especially the managers.

So, for today, can we start with 'Who?'. Take a look at these. As you can see, I've listed all the departments and teams into three groups. So, Group 1, is all the jobs and departments that require some or all of their staff to work at fixed times. This could include the call centre staff who are required to work shifts at fixed hours. Next, there's Group 2. These people will have to work core hours which are agreed by their line manager or team leader.

Karina What do you mean by 'core hours' exactly?

Paul So, core hours might be from 10.00 to 12.00 and 2.00 to 4.00. That person is required to be at their desk at those times, which gives them the flexibility to start earlier in the day or work later.

Karina So somebody could start work at 8.00 and finish at 4.00 or start at 10.00 and finish at 6.00?

Paul Exactly. What we need to avoid is a situation where everyone in a department starts work early and is leaving the building by 2.00 in the afternoon. This system should stop that from happening.

Maria But who's checking if they are in at 8.00, for example?

Paul Their manager.

Maria Yes, but what if the manager doesn't come in until 10.00?

Paul I'm dealing with that issue under 'What?' and 'How?'. So if we could come back to that later. Let's stay with 'Who?' for the moment.

So that's Group 2. And finally Group 3 tends to be middle and senior management – and they already work flexible hours. Now these are my initial groupings.

Karina Sorry, Paul, sorry, but I've got another meeting to go to – it started two minutes ago. I really have to go.

Paul Sure. I've overrun. We can continue with this next week. Can I ask you to take a look at these lists in the meantime and tell me if I need to change anything? Thanks.

MODULE 4

4.1

A This graph shows the revenues from sales for last year. Can everyone see it? Good, uh … Lester, could you go over the numbers for us?

B Sure. Um … as you can see, we had a pretty slow start last year. We sold 6,000 units in January, 6,000 in February …

C When did the spring sales campaign start?

B In March. You can see that sales rose slightly to 7,000, and then again in April – up to 8,000 units.

C Why did we have that dip in June?

B Ah. That was due to Lodgico.

C Lodgico?

A Our biggest competitor.

B Yeah, Lodgico launched a new product, and it cut into our market share. Sales fell to 5,000 units in May, and we dropped another thousand units in June.

C How did we deal with it?

B We increased our discounts to wholesalers. We got sales back to 5,000 in July and then 6,000 units in August. The dramatic rise came in the next two months. Sales jumped from 10,000 units in September to 13,000 in October.

C Was that because of holiday orders?

B That's right. And when the holiday orders stopped in November, sales went down by 6,000 units. They remained stable at 7,000 until the end of the year. Any more questions?

C Yes. What does the year-over-year comparison look like?

B OK. Here's last year's graph. Basically, there was a slight improvement in Q1 of this year compared to Q1 of last year – particularly in January and February.

4.2

A Overall sales are about the same as last year. The best-seller is ice-cream.

B But we've sold less of that than last year. Why's that?

75

AUDIO AND VIDEO SCRIPTS

A The market's changing. The cheaper multi-packs and standards are down, but the premiums are up. It's good because our margins are better on the more expensive brands.
B And look at the figures for yogurt!
A Yes, and yogurts have high margins, too.

4.3
A These figures are a little worrying.
B Why?
A Well, you can't see it here, but meat and poultry sales are lower than last year.
B And they account for almost half of our sales.
A Exactly.
B Do we know why?
A It might be part of a trend towards healthier eating. We're selling more vegetables.
B What about pizzas?
A They're doing very well. They're our fastest-growing product line.

4.4
B Pasta dishes are the most popular.
A Yes, they're still our best-sellers.
B This is a fast-growth market, right?
A Yes. We're offering a wider range, and consumers are becoming more adventurous. About half our sales are international recipes now.
B And curries?
A Yes, spicy dishes like curries are doing well. But the market's becoming more competitive, and some prices have come down.
B I'd like to see our market share compared with our competitors on these lines.

4.5
Mike So let's go through the figures for home sales this year. Tony?
Tony Thanks, Mike. Well, it's been a strange year so far. As you can see from the chart, sales were very good, excellent in fact, at the beginning of the year. They went up by 12.6% and we sold over 6,500 units between January and March, but then the next quarter was quite slow with an increase of only a disappointing 5.4%. This last, third quarter has been a bit better and sales are up by 9.2%.
However, the forecast for sales in the final quarter is just 7,050 units, an increase of only 4.7%, which means that we should end the year with an overall increase of under 8%. Short of our target, I'm afraid.
Mike Well, we'll have to discuss that later on this morning but let's hear about export sales now. Susan?

4.6
Mike Well, we'll have to discuss that later on this morning but let's hear about export sales now. Susan?
Susan Well, I'm very pleased to say that the export market is doing really well. As you know, the first two quarters this year were excellent with increases of 8.8% and a fantastic 15.4% over the same periods for last year. The sales figures for the last quarter have just come in and I'm delighted to tell you that we have been able to sell over 9,000 units for the first time in the history of the department, a great result which represents an increase of 11.4%. The forecast for the final quarter is also very promising. We expect an increase in sales of 13.5% with unit sales of 7,500, and that's a conservative estimate for the next three months which, if everything goes well, will mean an annual increase of 12.35% for this year, well over our initial target of 7.5%. Obviously, I'm really happy about the way the department has been working this year. We have done really well in eastern Europe and the new Madrid office has increased its sales by over 20% since January, which is a fantastic performance.
Now I'd like to mention a few people who …

4.7
Karl … So, that's all I want to say for the moment. Thank you very much for listening. Are there any questions?
Participant Yes. I understand that you can make the biodiesel fuel out of the jatropha plant, but can you explain the exact process? I mean, is it very complex?
Karl OK, thanks for your question. Actually, the basic procedure is fairly simple and has been possible for some time, but it's only in recent years that it's become economical. Essentially, there are two main stages: growing and processing. First of all, jatropha plants can be grown in hot climates and on poor land, so they are easier and cheaper to grow than many other types of vegetable biodiesel crops. When you are ready to harvest them, trucks pick up the seeds. Having brought the seeds to the refinery, you feed them into a grinder. Essentially, conversion to biodiesel is a one-stage process. Once the oil is taken out of the seeds – extracted – you're ready to mix it and heat it with methanol. Finally, you have a very good quality fuel and you can put it into any transport vehicle. And you also have a diesel engine which produces about half the CO_2 emissions of a normal diesel engine.

VIDEO 4
Extract 1
So, I'm here today to present you with the results of that survey. Now, to do this I've divided my presentation into three parts. Firstly, I'll talk about the background of the research. Then we'll look at how we approached the research, and thirdly I'll summarize the key findings of the research.
So, let's start with a brief description of the background. Six months ago, your company found that there was an increasing number of customers, in one of your company's three regions, that were cancelling their contracts within fourteen days. There were also a growing number of complaints to the call centre. So the key questions our survey needed to ask were: why so many complaints and why so many cancellations? Of course, there were also other issues that our survey needed to take into account …

Extract 2
So once we selected the 90,000 customers across your company's three regions, we then emailed them the survey. We allowed four weeks for them to respond to the surveys, and after that period we received a 4% response rate. Now this is quite good for this type of survey. We then analysed those responses and compiled them in a report for you. Let's look at these responses in a little bit more detail. Now of that 4%, this blue section shows that 57% of those responses came from the region with the difficulties. That's significant, as you are more likely to receive responses from customers who are either very satisfied or very unsatisfied. Anyway, this leads me on to the third and main part of my presentation: the actual results of the survey.
Now, in front of you, there's a handout with the survey's findings. I know you probably haven't had the time to study this in great detail, but what I'd like to do is give you an overview of the results, and talk about some issues for your customers.

Extract 3
I'm going to summarize the key findings for each of these questions. So let's begin with question one, which asks your customers how likely they are to recommend your company to a friend. As you can see, we have used a scale with one being not at all likely and ten being extremely likely. According to this chart, the overall response indicates that customers are fairly likely to recommend your company. However, this chart represents an average response across the three regions. If we break these responses down into the three regions

… like this, it illustrates the difference in customer satisfaction region by region. Now remember, red and yellow are the regions with increasing numbers of customers. Consequently, the responses are quite high – even as high as ten. But the lower scores in the previous chart were caused by the decline in these blue responses here. They go down to the zero level in some cases.

MODULE 6

6.1

Interviewer So tell us about CVs then, Marika. What are the key things to include?
Marika Well, you should start with brief personal details, of course. You know, name, age, and so on. Marital status is OK too, but no names of children or pets.
Interviewer And next comes education, I suppose?
Marika Yeah. You ought to list the schools and institutions you've attended in chronological order. Make sure that the dates make sense. Don't forget details of the qualifications you obtained. Remember to put down your grades too.
Interviewer I see. And would you advise people to include copies of their qualifications, and so on?
Marika No, they don't need to do that, not at this stage.
Interviewer Uh huh. Right. Now for the part of the CV which deals with work experience. Should we go through this in chronological order or start with the most recent, or current job first?
Marika I would definitely say begin with the present or most recent job first. Then work backwards. Give a brief description of each job and try to list one or two achievements.
Interviewer That's hard if you're still a student, isn't it?
Marika True, but you can still mention things like 'I was secretary of the Anglo-German Society' or give details of any part-time or holiday jobs.
Interviewer Oh, and one last question. What about a photograph?
Marika Well, it can go on an application form or with a covering letter, but there's no reason why you can't put it on your CV. If I were a job seeker, I'd invest in a studio photograph – one that made me look as good as possible, rather than one from a machine. And of course, never send a picture of you on the beach or at a party – people have sent me some amazing things!

VIDEO 5

Dacia My name is Dacia Henzell. I'm 31 and I'm from Trinidad and Tobago. I'm an electrical engineer by training. I've worked for the last five and a half years at Yara Trinidad Ltd as an electrical engineer. I've received a BSc in electrical and computer engineering from the University of the West Indies. Right now, at Cranfield, I'm studying for the full-time MBA.
Outside of work, I particularly like to spend my time playing tennis. I'm a little bit obsessed with it. So I look at the tournaments on TV, try to attend if I'm in the country that they're being held, and I … and I play a lot of tennis every week.
Yang My name is Yang Zeng and I'm from, originally from China. I came in the UK… came to the UK in 1999 and I did my undergraduate degree at University of Newcastle upon Tyne, and my major was in economics. And I … after I … after my degree I worked in the UK for six years. I worked in a private builders merchant based in the West Midlands called Carvers Wolverhampton and I worked as Overseas Procurement Manager for the company. I really enjoy socialize with my friends and also I'm quite active person. I usually go running and sometimes if I have time I will go surfing with my friends.
Adam My name is Adam Cox. I'm 35 years old and I'm from Australia.
Can you talk about your work experience?
Certainly. I have been self-employed all of my working life, for 18 years. I started my first business when I was 16 years old as a… as a record store owner on the Gold Coast in Australia. From there I opened a second store and a third. I sold the businesses off eight years later. I then went to create a tour management business which I subcontracted to quite a number of international record labels touring international and national artists all across Australia, and then from there I sold that business off and I started my own financial services and business consultancy firm, which I've owned for the last decade.
What qualifications do you have?
I did not finish high school. I do not have an undergrad. I have learnt pretty much all of my experience from practical application. I've attended a Harvard Business School executive education course in the last 12 months and now I'm undergoing my MBA at Cranfield.
And what interests and skills do you have?
I have quite a large interest in the music industry, having spent half of my professional career there. I enjoy quite a lot of sports and, most of all, I enjoy interacting with people, so being in a consultancy environment works very well with my personality.
Bryony My name is Bryony Smith and I'm a project manager. I've been a project manager in the telecommunications industry for nearly seven years. I've had quite a lot of professional training. I've had training in various different aspects of IT, I've had training in how to give good presentations, and I've also had training in effective communication. I've had some training in how to manage other members of staff and at the moment I manage a team of six people. In the past, I've also worked abroad so I speak fluent French and basic Spanish as well.

VIDEO 6

Maja Hello, Monica. Do have a seat.
Monica Thanks.
Paul So. Monica. Thanks for coming and for applying for the post of Finance Assistant, which of course is why Maja is also here. You two do know each other, don't you?
Maja Yes, I know Monica from reception but we've never really talked much, have we?
Monica No. But I know who you are.
Paul Good. Right. So, er … Thanks for filling in the application. Both myself and Maja have looked at it and what we'd like to do is ask you a few questions and, of course, give you time to ask us about the position. Although you already work here, in order to be fair we'll be structuring the interview in the same way as with an external applicant. Does that sound OK?
Monica Yes. Great.
Paul OK, so, did you get a chance to look at the job description I sent you?
Monica Yes, I did. I also spoke to Chloe Watson about it and she gave me a lot of information about what the job involves.
Paul Good. So basically we're looking for someone who can help Maja and her team with their day-to-day administrative requirements but also someone who can use their initiative and help the whole Finance Department as and when things come up.
Monica Yes, that's pretty much what Chloe said.

AUDIO AND VIDEO SCRIPTS

Paul Good. So can I start by asking why you applied for the job?

Monica Well, I thought it looked like an interesting job, and one that I could do well. I've been on reception for a while now and I never intended to stay there forever. So when I saw this position being advertised, I thought it would be a good opportunity to move up in the company.

Maja Would you say you're quite ambitious, then?

Monica Not especially, but I would like to do something a bit more challenging than reception.

Paul Can we talk a little more about your employment history now?

Maja Yes, I was looking at your CV and I saw that you worked with Reynolds and Waters – that's an accountancy firm, isn't it?

Monica Yes, that's right.

Maja What exactly were you doing for them?

Monica Well, it's a much smaller firm than this one so I did some reception work but I also acted as PA to three accountants. I was extremely busy and really had to learn to manage my time well.

Maja So why did you leave? Was it too much for you?

Monica No, not at all. I was on a temporary contract covering someone's maternity leave, so when she came back they had to let me go. No, I like being busy.

Paul Makes the time pass quicker, eh?

Monica No, I don't mean … It's just … it's nice to have a job where you can use your own initiative.

Maja That's interesting. And would you say you learned anything from working there that you could bring to this job?

Monica Well, as I said, time management skills. I also learned about accounting, and the kind of software used in finance, which I imagine would come in handy in this job.

Paul You mentioned using your initiative just now. Could you give us an example of a time when you have used your initiative? This could be with Reynolds and Waters or in your current position.

Monica Yes. One example would be just last week. I'd noticed that our regular courier service has been performing poorly recently, with packages being picked up late on more than a few occasions. So I took it upon myself to compile a list of alternative suppliers and their rates which I passed onto Karina to look into. I think that demonstrates me taking the initiative.

Maja And you did this without being asked?

Monica Yes, that's right.

Paul Let's talk a little more about the position itself. Maja – I'm sure you have some more questions to ask Monica.

Maja Yes, actually I wanted to tell you more about the job. It's a very demanding role. It's more than just basic office duties. The finance team needs someone they can rely on to organize the workload, deal with complicated data input …

Paul Yes, perhaps you could tell us what you think the biggest challenges would be and how you would overcome them.

Monica Right well, I imagine at the start the biggest challenge would be getting to grips with the processes and the software and things. But I'm a fast learner and I'm not afraid to ask questions if I need to.

Monica Um … I imagine once I'd been in the job for a while, the main challenge would be managing my time well … being able to do all the administrative jobs, as well as being your PA, Maja.

Maja And what do you think makes you the best candidate for the job?

Monica Um … well, I suppose my knowledge of the company makes me a stronger candidate than most people. Um … I'm very enthusiastic and I get on well with people which I imagine is important in this sort of job.

Paul OK. Well, thank you for answering our questions, Monica. We have five minutes left. Are there any questions you'd like to ask us?

Monica Yes, a couple of questions. Would I receive any kind of training for this job? For example, I saw in the job description it says I'll need to work with spreadsheets and basic software used in accounting. I'd need some help with that at the start.

Paul Maja? Could you answer that?

Maja Yes. I added that to the job description as something desirable rather than essential. So if we were to offer you the post obviously we'd make sure you got the necessary training.

Paul Anything else?

Monica Well, are the work conditions the same in an office job as on reception? Is it the same working hours, holiday …?

Paul Ah, good question. I would need to look at the terms of your current employment before I could answer that. There are some differences between the jobs. Ah, yes, I should have looked into that before I came in. Can I email you the answer later on?

Monica Yes, of course. Thanks.

Paul OK, great. If you have any other questions you know where to find me. OK? Good.

Maja Thanks for coming, Monica.

Monica Oh! There is one thing I forgot to ask. When will you know who's getting the job?

Paul We're interviewing two more people tomorrow and the day after so I'll be able to tell you by the end of the week.

Monica OK. Thanks.

Paul Thanks, Monica. Bye.

BEC 1

Linda Composource. Linda speaking. How can I help?

Gisele Good morning. My name is Gisele Kern from Abracomp in Germany. I'm following up an order I placed two weeks ago. I'd like to find out what has happened to it.

Linda I see. Can I take your account details?

Gisele Yes, the account reference is PG 278.

Linda I'm sorry, was that BJ?

Gisele No, 'P' for Peter, 'G' for George.

Linda OK, thanks. If you'll bear with me a moment, I'll call up your details. Let me see … So, when did you place the order?

Gisele On the 11th of February.

Linda Right, I've got it here. It was a repeat order for 2,000 motherboards. We put it straight through to our warehouse. According to my information, it was dispatched that afternoon.

Gisele Something must have gone wrong, because we haven't received them. I'm not happy about this at all. Could you check it out for me?

Linda Certainly, I'll look into it immediately. Would you like me to call you back, or will you hold while I contact the warehouse?

Gisele I think I'd better hold, because this is a real problem for me. I need this to be sorted out as soon as possible.

Linda I'll be as quick as I can.

Gisele Thanks. I really want to know what's happened to it.

BEC 2

Linda Hello, Ms Kern?

Gisele Yes. Still here.

Linda Sorry about the delay.

Gisele That's OK. So, have you found out about my order?

Linda Yes, I asked the warehouse to check what had happened to it. They told me it had gone two weeks ago.

Gisele Two weeks ago? Wait a moment, how did they send it?

Linda They said they'd sent it by sea.

Gisele By sea! But I always get my orders by international courier. I'm sure I told them to send it by courier when I placed the order.

Linda Let me look. Well you said asap, which I guess is by courier.

AUDIO AND VIDEO SCRIPTS

Gisele So where is it now?
Linda Well, I asked if they knew where it was. They said in a container in the ocean somewhere.
Gisele OK ... Well, in that case, can you send me 400 by courier? I need them urgently.
Linda Yes, of course. I'll deal with it immediately and get back to you within the hour. I'm very sorry about this.

BEC 3

Gisele You are through to Gisele Kern's voicemail. I'm not at my desk right now, so please leave a message after the beep.
Linda Ms Kern. It's Linda from Composource, calling at 3.30. I'm calling about the details of your order. We have sent 400 motherboards by courier today, the 26th of February. I told the courier to mark it top priority. They should be with you in two days. The reference number is HA 9872367, so you'll be able to track the parcel's progress. Once again, I'm very sorry for the problem with the original order. If you have any further problems, please don't hesitate to call me.

BEC 4

Presenter Thanks for coming today. As you know, we have a new customer database.
Staff Hurray!
Manager Well, nothing could be as slow as the old system!
Presenter Yes, well. As I say, the good news is we have a new database. But the bad news is that it will take a few weeks before we can use it in all our hotels. Now, it might seem a bit difficult to use at first, but in fact it's very simple. Your staff will need some training on how to use it. So the purpose of today is for you to start to become familiar with it. Now, up on the screen you can see what happens when you open the program. It looks very similar to the old database. But what's different, is this bottom half. As soon as you type in the details, it starts to suggest what kind of room the customer might like and what rooms are free. In other words, as well as giving the customer more of what they want, it also makes it quicker to process a booking for a regular customer and give them their favourite room.
Manager Will it let me make notes on the client?
Presenter Yes, you can type notes into this section for future reference. For example, if you want to advertise a special promotion to male customers over the age of forty, then it'll tell you who they are.
Manager How does it know what to match?
Presenter It has these drop-down menus, which allow you to categorize the information when the booking is taken. The more detailed the information, the better the match. So, on the one hand, it'll take you more time to get the information, but on the other hand, we think it'll save time later on.
Manager So what happens when the customer doesn't want to tell you their age, for example?
Presenter Well, obviously one downside is that you can't demand the information. But on the plus side, the customer can book online now, and hopefully they'll give us the extra information then. In other words, the more they tell us, the quicker the booking is next time they call ...

BEC 5

Carmen Now our aim is to make the move as smooth as possible. What's happening with the office space, Erica?
Erica Well, everything is going according to plan. We expect to be ready on schedule.
Carmen That's great. Where are we with the revised department structure?
Dieter That's under control too. We just need to put in the finishing touches.
Carmen Fantastic. Great work, everyone. Now, Nikos, tell us about your plans.
Nikos Thanks, Carmen. Well, as we know, a lot of mergers are unsuccessful because of a 'two-camps' mentality.
Dieter To a certain extent this is inevitable.
Nikos Yes, but we hope to reduce problems to a minimum.
Carmen I agree. So where does this leave us?
Nikos Well, over the next few weeks, I plan to hold a series of small meetings, say over coffee, where people can meet informally and develop a relationship.
Erica That's a good idea. They'll get to know each other before working together. How long will it take to involve all the staff?
Nikos Well, I intend to have seven or eight sessions.
Carmen What's the timescale on this?
Nikos To involve everyone? By the end of next month.
Carmen Mm. So, what's the next step?
Nikos Well, before I can finalize the arrangements, I need a list of Buckler's key people.
Erica I'll prepare a list this afternoon.
Nikos Great. Then we can liaise, and we should have a schedule by Tuesday.
Carmen Good. We're also going to organize a big event for everybody. I'd like it to be fun, so if anyone has any ideas, I would be extremely grateful.
Dieter Perhaps Nikos and I could work on this together.
Carmen That's an excellent idea. Anyway, let's not forget that it is likely that there'll be a few problems in the short term, but the chances are there won't be too many personality clashes in the long run. I'm confident that with careful handling the process will be pretty smooth.

BEC 6

Interviewer You're an independent computer manufacturer. That's right, isn't it?
Steve Yes, that's right. We make up machines to our customers' specifications.
Interviewer So you're a bit like Dell, then?
Steve If only! We're tiny by comparison. But we believe that customers like the personal touch. We can spend a lot of time discussing their needs and the type of machine they need. And if there's a problem, they don't have to send the machine away, they just come to the shop. Of course, we don't have Dell's advantages – that is, in terms of their suppliers – so we have to keep a lot of components in stock.
Interviewer How do you make sure that you don't run out?
Steve Well, everything has its own bar code which shows up on the database. It tells us what we have left, if it's on order, and so on – see?
Interviewer Right. Obviously, you never want to run out of basic items.
Steve That's right – it's really not good to be out of stock.
Interviewer So, does the database automatically place an order if you're running low on something?
Steve No, it just warns us we're low on stock. You don't want to stock up on components which are going to become obsolete.
Interviewer OK. Now, a lot of your components come from Asia, don't they?
Steve That's right. We generally have them sent by an international courier.
Interviewer So, do you take advantage of the tracking facility?
Steve It depends, really. I mean, if something's not particularly urgent, then I don't bother. But if there's an essential package, I keep track of it very closely.

OXFORD
UNIVERSITY PRESS

Great Clarendon Street, Oxford, OX2 6DP, United Kingdom

Oxford University Press is a department of the University of Oxford.
It furthers the University's objective of excellence in research, scholarship,
and education by publishing worldwide. Oxford is a registered trade
mark of Oxford University Press in the UK and in certain other countries

© Oxford University Press 2012

The moral rights of the author have been asserted

First published in 2012

2019
10

No unauthorized photocopying

All rights reserved. No part of this publication may be reproduced, stored
in a retrieval system, or transmitted, in any form or by any means, without
the prior permission in writing of Oxford University Press, or as expressly
permitted by law, by licence or under terms agreed with the appropriate
reprographics rights organization. Enquiries concerning reproduction outside
the scope of the above should be sent to the ELT Rights Department, Oxford
University Press, at the address above

You must not circulate this work in any other form and you must impose
this same condition on any acquirer

Links to third party websites are provided by Oxford in good faith and for
information only. Oxford disclaims any responsibility for the materials
contained in any third party website referenced in this work

ISBN: 978 0 19 473979 5   Student's Book
ISBN: 978 0 19 473980 1   DVD
ISBN: 978 0 19 473978 8   Pack

Printed in China

This book is printed on paper from certified and well-managed sources

ACKNOWLEDGEMENTS

Material for Business Essentials taken and adapted from the following sources:
Business Focus Pre-intermediate, by David Grant and Robert McLarty;
Business Objectives International edition, by Vicki Hollett; Business One:One
Pre-intermediate, by Rachel Appleby, John Bradley, Brian Brennan, and Jane
Hudson; Business One:One Intermediate, by Rachel Appleby, John Bradley,
Brian Brennan, and Jane Hudson; Business Result Pre-intermediate, by David
Grant and Jane Hudson; Business Result Intermediate, by John Hughes and
Jon Naunton; Business Result Teacher's website, by Gareth Davies, John
Hughes, and Shaun Wilden; Commerce 1, by Martyn Hobbs and Julia Starr
Keddle; Commerce 2, by Martyn Hobbs and Julia Starr Keddle; Profile 2, by
Jon Naunton; Successful Presentations, by John Hughes and Andrew Mallett;
Successful Meetings, by John Hughes and Andrew Mallett

The publisher would like to thank the following for their kind permission to reproduce photographs and other copyright material: Alamy pp.5 (Luc Novovitch), 7 (Ben Molyneux), 10 (moodboard), 18 (drinking/Paul Bradbury), 24 (bag/Nicholas Eveleigh), 25 (website/Jan Miks), 25 (child/Picture Partners), 25 (phone/pixelbully), 26 (keys/Colouria Media), 26 (id/Corbis Flirt), 47 (Glow Asia RF); Getty Images pp.2 (walking/Image Source), 13 (Ariel Skelley), 14 (Fotografia By Cris Zuin), 17 (Image Source), 25 (parcel/KAI-UWE KNOTH/AFP), 33 (Abel Mitja Varela); Glasbau Hahn p.20 (Royal Ontario Museum, Toronto, © 2006 Richard Johnson Photography Inc.); Oxford University Press pp.2 (coffee/Stockbyte), 2 (woman/Somos), 9 (White), 12 (Stockbyte), 15 (ImageState), 18 (speech/Hill Street Studios), 18 (dinner/Nick White), 23 (Heidi/Moodboard), 23 (Sara/Radius Images), 26 (numberpad/Digital Vision), 27 (Gareth Boden), 35 (Gareth Boden), 40 (sellotape/Dennis Kitchen Studio, Inc), 40 (post-its/Corbis), 44 (James Hardy), 50 (Gareth Boden); Shutterstock pp.18 (meeting/Monkey Business Images), 23 (Benjamin/Tyler Olson), 24 (razor/bart78), 26 (swipe card/gifted), 40 (pen/Lipik), 40 (highlighters/graja), 48 (Goodluz); Thinkstock pp.2 (computer/Stockbyte), 4 (Fuse), 6 (Design Pics), 16 (George Doyle), 19 (Thomas Northcut), 21 (Rayes), 22 (Hemera), 24 (chair/iStockphoto), 24 (bulb/iStockphoto), 36 (Brand X Pictures)

Illustrations by: Ian Baker/Cartoon Stock p.38; Ed McLachlan p.49; Willie Ryan/Illustration p.34